A Call to Prayer

A 31-Day Prayer Devotional

Global Compass Prayer Ministries, Inc., and Friends

DULUTH, GA

Copyright © 2025 by **Fay Scott Gordon and Global Compass Prayer Ministries, Inc.**

All rights reserved. This book is protected by the copyright laws of the United States of America. This book may not be copied or reprinted for commercial gain or profit. No copies of this book or any parts of this book can be reprinted or disseminated in any form, including electronic, mechanical, photocopy, recording, or otherwise, unless you have prior written permission from the publisher. Permission may be granted upon request.

A Call to Prayer
Global Compass Prayer Ministries, Inc.
Fay Scott Gordon, Founder
Diana Treadwell, Co-Founder
http://globalcompassprayerministries.com

Published by **Rain Publishing**
https://rainpublishing.com
info@rainpublishing.com

Cover Design by **Sheldon Rollins**
Contact Sheldon at srproductions@gmail.com
404.302.7038

Unless otherwise noted, all scriptures are taken from the New International Version Bible, the New King James Version Bible, and the New Living Translation Bible.

A Call to Prayer/Fay Scott Gordon, Global Compass Prayer Ministries, Inc.
First edition.

ISBN: 979-8-9927864-2-2

Library of Congress Control Number: 2025914033

Dedicated to the memory of the late Evangelist Toby Gordon and Pastor Kenneth A. Flowers

Evangelist Toby Gordon inspired the start of Global Compass Prayer Ministries. He was known for saying, "We are behind enemy lines," and lived his life as a warrior evangelizing, preaching, and teaching the word of God.

Pastor Kenneth A. Flowers Jr. left a legacy with Global Compass Prayer Ministries that cannot be erased. He demonstrated the Word of God in action by ministering to us and consistently speaking into our lives.

Acknowledgements

Deep gratitude goes to the company of Intercessory prayer leaders and those who get up early to enter His gates with thanksgiving and His courts with praise on behalf of others around the world through prayer. Your constant prayers, support, and never-ending encouragement sustained us over the years to continue to do what God has called us to do.

Many thanks to Pastor Marc S. Bryant, Pastor Evans Pierre, Reverend Margie Fleurant, and Pastor Dewayne Wright, who never said no to advising, supporting, and speaking into our lives, and to the many others who always supported our Prayer Summits by showing up and praying.

To our publisher, Rachel Renee Griggs of Rain Publishing, and our digital designer, Sheldon Rollins of SR Productions, because of you, I was confident of the outcome of this project. Thank you for your professionalism and expertise in the smooth completion of this book.

Contents

Part I - The Importance of Intercession

1- Take Your Place in the Kingdom of God – Fay Scott Gordon..........1
2- The Prayer of Intercession – Margie Fleurant......................5
3- Flourish Like a Tree – Veronica Gay-Brown........................11
4- Ask, Seek, and Knock! – Lakeisha Osbourne-Cannon 15
5- God – Beverly A. Sylvester.......................................17
6- Your Prayers Are Heard -Dr. Carla Palin..........................21
7- Bold Prayer – Dr. Tricia Robinson...............................25
8- Don't Doubt God – Dr. Veronica M. Ambrose 29
9- Watch and Pray in Faith – Rev. Adrianne Smiling.................35
10- Victory Over Trials and Tribulations – Elder Crystal R. Steward....39

Part II - Prayer Changes Things

11- If it Wasn't True, He Would Have Told Me – Stephanie Torrey......45
12- My Source – Diana Treadwell 49
13- Growing in Love – Jannie Broxton 51
14- Strength for the Journey – Elder Kim R. Hernandez 57
15- Faith. Favor. Freedom – Michele B. Thompson....................63
16- Look Up to God – Vernesa Penny Green 67
17- Let Go and Let God – Carol Raftis..............................71
18- A Woman and a Well – Rev. Easter Frazier.......................75
19- Manifest! Manifest! Manifest! – Dr. Merilyn V. Davis...........81
20- Abandoned but not Forgotten – Diana Stevens....................83
21- Trust the Lord – Darcel Lowery.................................87

Part III - The Life of an Intercessory Prayer Warrior

22-Trusting God in A Challenging Time – Dr. Claire P. Higgins.......... 93
23-Small Group Praying – Pastor Freddie Williams............................... 99
24-Living in Peace on Purpose – Linda B. Johnson 103
25-The Perfect Quilt of Prayer With Jesus - Ellen Carter Haygood.. 109
26-Behind the Fog - the Word of God – Ruby Warthen 115
27-Our Code Foundation -Dr. Elsie L. Scott... 119
28-Jesus Wept! – Leslie K. Powell Pitchford... 123
29-The Fullness of God – Earnestine Porter 127
30-Renewed Like an Eagle – Evang. Ida Flowers................................ 129
31-Making a Transition from Belief to Faith: Strategies of Heaven – Pastor Kenneth A. Flowers 133
A Prayer for Salvation 139

Foreword

One of the key realities to having a successful Christian journey is establishing a devotional life. Unfortunately, many do not possess such knowledge and understanding of one. Our modern context in the twenty-first century requires us to regain some lost truths and disciplines that provided earlier generations with the tools that lent to a positive Christian journey. What Global Compass Prayer Ministries, led by Fay Scott Gordon, has produced in this devotional book is to provide the Body of Christ with a tool that helps believers develop and grow in their relationship with the Lord, so that their journey can be a successful one. This devotional resource will motivate the believer to engage in the discipline of prayer.

It is important to understand the meaning of the term devotional, from the root word "devote." The Online Etymology Dictionary provides the root understanding of the term as shown below.

c. 1200, devocioun, "profound religious emotion, awe, reverence," from Old French devocion "devotion, piety" and directly from Latin devotionem (nominative devotio), noun of action from past-participle stem of devovere "dedicate by a vow, sacrifice oneself, promise solemnly," from, de "down, away" (see de-) + vovere "to vow" (see vow (n.)). From late 14c. as "an act of religious worship, a religious exercise" (now usually devotions). In ancient Latin, "act of consecrating by a vow," also "loyalty, fealty, allegiance;" in Church Latin, "devotion to God, piety."[1]

From the etymological definitions presented above, one observes that the term has a religious orientation. The Bible postulates devotion as one's loyalty, fealty, or allegiance to God.

Also, it is one's sacrificial vow to do something or perform a particular act. Furthermore, a person perceives it as sacrificially pursuing communion with God through various spiritual disciplines, such as Scripture meditation and prayer.

The purpose of a devotional is to promote and facilitate communion with God by granting the worshipper guidance and structure. This is exactly what this devotional on prayer is for. As one reads the chapters of this book, they receive information that helps them to better commune with the Lord. As people engage this material, they will find that their time with the Lord is more scriptural and lends itself to a successful journey in Christ.

Global Compass Prayer Ministries, Inc. has committed to interceding on behalf of the church and the world for over two decades. They have led conferences on the subject matter of prayer and intercession. They have established intercessional hubs throughout the world in the hopes of fanning a global flame for intercession. They now perceive the need to stretch beyond their present ministerial scope to where they are creating and providing material that will assist the Church to better execute the ministry of intercession through devotional materials. This shows their level of commitment to God and to you, the reader, in seeking your edification regarding prayer.

My hope for this devotional book is that you, the reader, will find within its pages content that will not only provide you with knowledge and understanding but will stir within your own heart to enter the depths of the ministry of intercession. God spoke to Ezekiel, saying, "'So I sought for a man among them who would make a wall and stand in the gap before Me on behalf of the land, that I should not destroy it, but I found no one. Therefore, I have poured out My indignation on them; I have consumed them with the fire of My wrath; and I have recompensed their deeds on their own heads,' says the Lord God."[2] Because God could not find an intercessor, one who stands in the gap, He brought judgment upon the nation of Israel. This is a profound thought.

When we consider the Old Testament, there have been various people identified as intercessors who stood in the gap. One of those very people was Moses. When God said He would destroy the twelve tribes, Moses stood in the gap, pleading for Israel.[3] Another person was Samuel. When the Philistines sought to come against the people of Israel, Samuel interceded on their behalf. God heard his prayer, and He defeated the Philistines in a supernatural way.[4] This is the power of prayer/intercession!

This devotional resource will be one of several powerful books in circulation because of its intended purpose. This devotional book intends to help you not only learn about prayer, but to promote you becoming an intercessor, who effectively stands in the gap before God on behalf of others. May God richly bless you as you process through this devotional. Your life will never be the same!

~Prophet Evans Pierre, Senior Leader of Kingdom Insight Church

---

1. Online Etymology Dictionary, s.v., "devotion," accessed February 19, 2025, https://www.etymonline.com/word/devotion.
2. Ezekiel 22:30-31 (NKJV)
3. Exodus 32:7-14
4. 1 Samuel 7:7-14

Prophet Evans Pierre is a devoted messenger of the Gospel, a profound teacher of God's Word, a prophetic officer, and a gifted author. With an unwavering commitment to his calling, he serves as the Senior Pastor at Kingdom Insight Church, located in the vibrant community of Edison, NJ.

Evans is not only a faithful steward of the Word but also a lifelong learner. He earned his bachelor's degree from Nyack College. He furthered his theological journey by attaining a Master of Divinity from Regent University, equipping him with the knowledge and insight to lead God's people.

In line with the biblical mandate to prepare and empower the saints for ministry, Evans holds a deep conviction that his purpose is to equip the Body of Christ for effective service. Wherever he goes, he carries the torch of knowledge and imparts the wisdom necessary to fulfill this sacred mission.

Beyond his pastoral duties, Evans finds his greatest joy in being a devoted husband to Christina and a loving father to their cherished daughters, Janisa and Janelle. These roles, he believes, are an extension of his ministry, reflecting the love and grace of God in his own home.

In Prophet Evans Pierre, Kingdom Insight Church has a shepherd who not only leads with passion and wisdom but also strives to illuminate the path of faith for all who seek to walk in the light of God's Word.

Introduction

Global Compass Prayer Ministries, Inc. is a group of believers who have embraced salvation and were drawn together because we love and understand the importance of Intercessory Prayer, and we are determined to fulfill the call of God on our lives. We sharpen each other with the gifts, talents, and abilities that we have by praying and encouraging each other to reach our highest level in God. This devotional was created to inspire and influence all who read it to gain an understanding and level of appreciation of the individuality and unity of prayer at the same time. While we engage in corporate prayer, we make sure to pray to God and not to each other. We realize that we all have different experiences, which lead us to different depths in prayer. Enjoy the devotions that God used in this book to inspire you.

~Fay Scott Gordon, Founder of Global Compass Prayer Ministries, Inc.

The Importance of Intercession

Global Compass
Prayer Ministries Inc.

Take Your Place in the Kingdom of God

Fay Scott Gordon

My favorite attribute about God is that He is Sovereign and He presides over every event, great or small. He is always in control, it doesn't always look like it, doesn't always feel like it, but He is. He is all-powerful, He is all-mighty, He is the beginning, He is the end. He is the same yesterday, today, and forever, and there is no comparison to Him.

My second favorite attribute about Him is how He loves me, He knows me, and is acquainted with all my ways. I can't go anywhere from Him; even if I were to make my bed in hell, He is there. His thoughts towards me are more in number than the sand, and every hair on my head is numbered. He fearfully and wonderfully made me in my mother's womb and made good plans for me that will always bring me to victory because He works all things together for my good. He sent His only Son to die for me, and through Him will do all things for me. Because of all these things and so many more, I don't want His dying to be in vain in my life. I plan to fulfill every plan He has for me.

Yes, I plan to take the place that He planned for me in the kingdom of God. I want to fit in where I belong to accomplish His will for me in my life and on the earth. The life of the family that He placed me in, the ministry that He anointed and designed for me to help and influence others with. I plan to be the light, the salt, and the witness that I am supposed to be as I lift up the name of Jesus.

I strive to do these things by believing who He says He is and who He says I am. I endeavor to do these things through the faith that He has given me by daily keeping an emphasis on prayer. I realize that the most important area of my relationship with God is prayer, which is merely communication. In any relationship, good communication is key. For instance, communication between a husband and wife is crucial to a good relationship. Good communication between parents and their children can prevent harm, danger, and mistakes. This holds true in any relationship.

One of the greatest forms of worship to God is to find yourself doing what He has called you to do; to be in pursuit of His will for your life. For years after I accepted Christ, I asked God what I was called to do. Looking back over my life, I realized that I was not perfect by a long shot, but I kept doing what I knew was right. I started going to church, I separated myself from my worldly friends, I even stopped wearing pants for a while because that's what I was taught. Plenty of times I missed the mark, but I kept loving, forgiving, giving, and praying the best I knew. Prayer, the word, and a desire to please God kept me connected to Him.

Along the way I discovered some hindrances from within and from the outside...... such as fear, discouragement, depending on others who put me into their box rather than seeking God for myself, not maintaining the relationship with God needed to know His voice and follow His lead, not really believing what the word said about me, getting so caught up in my own ambitions and desires that I ignored His leading. Finally, I realized that God is a good parent, and He doesn't tell me to do anything He hasn't equipped me to do. As I grow older and continue to mature in my relationship with Him, I realize that His plans for me to do what

He called me to do are ongoing and as I continue to seek Him daily, I fit into His plans for me.

For some of us, doing what God has called us to can be the thing we have been doing from childhood, and as we mature, the responsibility of it matures. For others, it involves our vocation and our education. Some are called to simply train our children in the way they should go, or to be the best supportive spouse, or be the best example of a Christian we can be. Sometimes it may not be the handwriting on the wall; you may already do it and love it.

Doing what God has called you to do may have nothing to do with a specific title, or a specific position in church, at work, or community; it could just be the significance of being you. God's plan for us makes the world go round for us and others, no matter what it is. Sometimes people specifically get paid a salary to do what God calls them to do, and sometimes not. However, the rewards are more than you can imagine. When you are doing what God has called you to do, you may be overwhelmed with a feeling of importance, contentment, thankfulness, and gratitude without pride; in fact, it humbles you. It can truly be your happy place. The rewards are great on earth and in heaven.

If you want to hear from God concerning your place in His kingdom, pray, fast, and study scriptures that pinpoint hearing God's voice. Focus on the concept of God speaking through His Word, the Holy Spirit, and through the guidance of conscience, as well as emphasizing the importance of seeking God's wisdom and listening to His guidance.

> *Father God, I welcome you into every moment, every day of my life. I don't want to live on my own, knowing that your ways are better than mine. You said that your thoughts towards me are more in number than the sand, and wherever I am, you are there. Father God, you are the very air that I breathe, and I am actively seeking Your direction for my life to live, be, and do all that You have planned for me. Amen.*

Scripture references: Psalm 139, Ephesians 1:11, Hebrews 12:2, Colossians 4:2, Jeremiah 29:11, Psalm 32:8, Romans 8:32, Jeremiah 1:5, Psalm 37:5, Ephesians 2:10

Fay Scott Gordon is the founder of Global Compass Prayer Ministries and has enjoyed mobilizing intercessors over the years to accomplish the Great Commission by winning the lost to Christ as we go around the world interceding, equipping, and instructing believers to grow to maturity by fulfilling the call of God on their lives with an emphasis on prayer. My greatest accomplishments are accepting Jesus Christ as my Lord and Savior, my three lovely daughters Keisha, Jewel, and Alease, and my five beautiful grandchildren, Emmanuel, David, Mia, Ty, and Demetrius Jeh.

The Prayer of Intercession

Margie Fleurant

What is the Prayer of Intercession, and what is an Intercessor? The Prayer of Intercession is a prayer for another. It's not praying for yourself. It's praying for another person. It's standing in the gap, putting up the hedge on behalf of another person.

> I sought for a man among them who would stand in the gap before God. Ezekiel 22:30

As an Intercessor, you're praying for another person. An Intercessor is a mediator. Webster's Dictionary defines it as "A go-between; an intercessor, one who interposes between two parties and acts as a mediator for the purpose of reconciling them." This is very exciting, especially as we go into this. We're going to talk later on about how you can stand in the gap on behalf of someone who is not aligned with Jesus Christ, doesn't know Him as their Lord and Savior, and you're going to see the power of your prayers and how the effectual fervent prayer of a righteous man avails much.

The devil hates Intercessors. I remember Kenneth E. Hagin teaching one time on The Prayer of Intercession, and one time he was casting the devil out of somebody. As the demons were coming out of the person, they were screaming, "I hate Intercessors. I hate Intercessors." So, that just goes to show you the power of your prayers. I was thinking, you know, I wonder if somebody, somewhere maybe a mother, a father, a grandfather, whoever was praying for that person that was delivered, and it was that very prayer that broke the power of the evil spirit and that very prayer that caused that person to go up in that prayer line because when you pray for someone, it makes the crooked ways straight and the rough places plain and causes things to work together according to Divine Order and the purposes of God. Prayer opens up the door for God to work. So, God only knows, if that demon was screaming, "I hate Intercessors," somebody was probably praying for that individual and lifting them up with the idea of completely removing the scruple of conscience off of them so they could be in a position to be delivered and set free.

I believe that in the realm of the Spirit, there's a lot we don't see, and there's a lot we don't know, but what we do know is that prayer works. And so, we've got to be steadfast, immovable, always abounding in the work of prayer, knowing that our labors are not in vain.

And you can't give up. Jesus said in His word, "Men ought to always pray and not faint." You can't give up when you're praying the Prayer of Intercession. We're going to get into this, but I'm yielding to the Holy Ghost, and that's what I do when I teach. I have my notes, but I yield, and then we get back.

You can't give up! Oftentimes, things get a whole lot worse before they get a whole lot better. When you begin to pray The Prayer of Intercession on behalf of a person, a nation, whatever the case may be, a leader, sometimes things get worse before they get better. Why? Because prayer opens up the door for God to work. So, if you're praying for an unsaved person, then that unsaved person gets uncomfortable. The demons that are operating in or around that person are getting agitated because, in the realm of the Spirit, you're putting pressure on the enemy, and he doesn't want to give up his stronghold.

Do you remember the story of the time when Jesus cast the devil out of that little boy? Remember that story? Okay. What happened before the demons left the little boy? He put up a big stink, made a big, loud noise, tore him, and then left. In other words, the devil put up a big stink. He knew he had to go, but he had to put on a show. Isn't that just like our enemy?

So, from Webster's, here is another definition of an Intercessor: to plead or make a request on behalf of another; to intervene with the purpose of producing agreement. Remember that.

The Greek word means to get the heir of a king on the behalf of another. Who is the King of Kings and Lord of Lords? Our God. Amen! He reigns. He is high and lifted up. He is our King. So, as an Intercessor, we're getting his ear on behalf of another person. And how many of you know that God hears you when you pray?

The Prayer of Intercession is the greatest act of love you can do for anybody. Jesus said in John 15:12-13, "This is my commandment: That you love one another as I have loved you." And then He goes on to say, "Greater love has no man than this, that a man would lay down his life for his friend."

Jesus came to the earth as an Intercessor (Isaiah 59:16). He bridged the gap between God and sinful man. He was the Intercessor. Are you listening?

So, what He's saying in this scripture is that the greatest act of love you can do for someone is to lay down your life and give your time to the Prayer of Intercession on behalf of another person.

I've been on assignment for many, many, many leaders throughout my walk with God since I learned about The Prayer of Intercession, and what God showed me was, we think that it's the preacher doing all the work and oh, he's so anointed or she's so anointed. And, oh, the preacher was hot on fire. But nobody knows about the intercessors that are in the backroom, hiding in the closet, so to speak, and standing in the gap, and praying on behalf of that leadership. And because prayer opens up the door for God to work, it opens up the door for people to be saved and come to the knowledge of the truth. It opens up the door for signs, wonders, and miracles. It opens up the door for that leader to be so anointed. Yes, they studied to show themselves approved unto God. Yes, they do what's right. But do you know that when you pray for them, it causes a fresh fire and a fresh anointing to come upon them? Are you listening? So, it is the greatest act of love.

Hebrews 7:24-25 says, "That we have a high-priest…" -Jesus. The Bible says, "He ever lives to make intercession." He what? "He ever lives to make intercession."

So, the Ministry of Intercession is a continual, priestly ministry. But the Intercessor, Jesus, is on the inside of you. And what we need to do is release Jesus, the Intercessor. He is longing to flow through you. He's longing to flow through me. But we have to yield to Him, and we have to say yes.

> As he is, so are we in this world. 1 John 4:17
>
> I'm crucified with Christ. It is no longer I who live, but Christ lives in me. Galatians 2:20

The Intercessor is on the inside of you. He ever lives to make intercession, and He needs to be loosed and let go. I like this definition. Intercession involves taking hold of God's will, His word, and His promises and refusing to let go until His will comes to pass. That's why we call it the Art of Intercession.

> Be steadfast, immovable, always abounding in the work of prayer, knowing that your labors are not in vain. 1 Corinthians 15:58

Margie Fleurant is the founder of Margie Fleurant Ministries and the President of The River Ministries. She is dedicated to equipping the body of Christ, and training people to develop intimacy with God. With the use of media, which includes Charisma Podcast, Kingdom 1st TV, and other social media avenues, Margie is able to better reach the nations with the call to prayer and intercession. Margie is a passionate teacher who uses the prophetic gifts God has given her to teach on faith, intercession, and the importance of intimacy with God.

Margie has been in full-time ministry for over 40 years. She graduated from Rhema Bible Training College (1977) and is an ordained minister. Margie is the author of ten books, including Focus and Encountering God Through Prayer, both of which are published by Destiny Image Publishers and are available in bookstores and online. You can find Margie's books, teachings, and other resources on her website at www.margiefleurant.org.

Flourish Like a Tree

Veronica Gay-Brown

As one begins his/her Christian journey, it is important to remember that you are "A New Creation." You must nurture and immerse yourself in the Word of God. Study the basic principles of Christianity; surround yourself with men and women of God who help you become a better person, help you to learn and grow, and help you to stay focused. Once you establish yourself and become rooted and grounded in the love of God, nurture yourself and feed on the Word of God and the Promises of God. Eventually, you will begin to blossom into that unique expression of God, illuminating His light, His love, His creativity, His brilliance, His understanding, His peace, and his protection.

THE SOUL OF A TREE
THE HUMAN SPIRIT
GENTLE, TENDER, BEAUTIFUL, AND GRACIOUS
LIKE THE CHERRY BLOSSOM TREE

THE HUMAN SPIRIT
PEACEFUL, SERENE, AND CALM
LIKE THE PALM TREE

THE HUMAN SPIRIT
APPEARING SAD BUT EXUDING STRENGTH AND STABILITY
LIKE THE WEEPING WILLOW TREE

THE HUMAN SPIRIT
BRIGHT, ENTHUSIASTIC, COLORFUL, AND FREE SPIRITED
LIKE THE RED LEAF MAPLE TREE

THE HUMAN SPIRIT
FIERY, AMBITIOUS, AND PASSIONATE
LIKE THE AUTUMN BLAZE TREE

THE HUMAN SPIRIT
COMFORTING AND PROTECTIVE
LIKE THE AMERICAN OAK TREE
TREES
THEY GIVE US LIGHT, LOVE, AND PURPOSE

GOD EXPRESSES HIMSELF
THROUGH THE HUMAN SPIRIT
THROUGH NATURE

Dear Heavenly Father God,

I come before the throne of grace each morning thanking you for waking me up with a mind to pray. Thank you, Father God, for creating in me a clean heart and renewing my mind and my spirit. Thank you, Father God for the Promises of your Word. Thank you, Father God, for providing all my needs according to your riches and glory. Thank you, Father God, for allowing me to use my gifts and creativity to draw others closer to you.

> The righteous will flourish like a palm tree, they will grow like a cedar of Lebanon; planted in the house of the Lord, they will flourish in the courts of our God. They will bear fruit in old age; they will stay fresh and green. Psalm 92: 12-14
>
> The person is like a tree planted by streams of water, which yields its fruit in season and whose leaf does not wither - whatever they do prospers. Psalm 1:3
>
> She is a tree of life to those who take hold of her; those who hold fast will be blessed. Proverbs 3:18
>
> On each side of the river stood the tree of life, bearing twelve crops of fruit. And the leaves of the tree are for the healing of nations. Revelations 22:2

For further study, please read and meditate on the following scriptures:
- 1 Corinthians 13:4-6
- 1 Corinthians 13:13
- Psalm 37:4
- Jeremiah 29:11
- Galatians 5:22
- Matthew 6:33
- Matthew 22:37
- Philippians 4:8

Veronica and her husband have been studying and serving at Faith Christian Outreach Center, under Pastor W.W. Robinson, in Plainfield, New Jersey, for over 20 years. Veronica has taught Children's Bible Study for over 10 years and is a committed Prayer Leader of F.C.O.C.'s Prayer Ministry. In addition, Veronica has been a member of the Global Compass Intercessory Prayer Ministry for over 10 years.

Veronica is employed with the Plainfield School District and considers her work ministry. She serves as a Teacher Assistant, Substitute Teacher, Librarian, and Gifted and Talented Teacher in the after-school program. Her corporate background includes working for Avon Books/Hearst Corporation as a freelance writer.

Veronica graduated from Kean University with a master's degree in public administration. She graduated Cum Laude with a 3.67 GPA, and was inducted into the Phi, Alpha, Alpha National Honor Society. Prior to graduating, Veronica was awarded the Mayor's Community Service Award.

In her spare time, Veronica enjoys spending time with her family, reading, listening to music, nature-walking, and philanthropic activities.

Ask, Seek, and Knock!

Lakeisha Osborne-Cannon

Prayer is our greatest privilege as Christians and is vital to our relationship with God. By having a personal connection with God, I have learned that Prayer is more than just a ritual or a set of words; it's a personal conversation with God. Looking back over my life, I can recall the moments when God listened closely to my prayers and answered miraculously. In my walk with the Lord, I have also learned that prayer has the power to change situations and hearts. It allows us to tap into God's endless resources and boundless love. No request is too small; no problem is too big for God to handle. In the chapter of Matthew, verse 7, we find Jesus stating,

> Ask, and it will be given to you; seek, and you will find; knock, and it will be opened to you. For everyone who asks receives, and he who seeks finds, and to him who knocks it will be opened. Matthew Chapter 7:7-8

In these verses, Jesus teaches His disciples to trust God's goodness by persistently asking and seeking Him through prayer. In His statement, our Lord addresses all difficulties by promising that it will be given to us if we ask Him for anything in prayer. We can be assured that no forces can hinder the fulfillment of the Lord's word. The phrase "I say unto you" should eliminate all our doubts forever when we approach the Lord in prayer. What an uplifting and freeing teaching!

Whether you're asking, seeking, or knocking in prayer to God for guidance, provision, forgiveness, or strength, remember that you're not talking to an impersonal force but to a loving Father who knows our needs and desires the best for us.

> *Father, help me to be persistent in prayer and steadfast in bringing my requests before You. Teach me to stand in faith in Jesus when I pray. Forgive me for wimpy prayers and empower me to pray with the boldness of the Holy Spirit. Teach me how to continually ask, seek, and knock. In Jesus' name, I pray. Amen.*

> Ask, and it will be given to you; seek, and you will find; knock, and it will be opened to you. For everyone who asks receives, and he who seeks finds, and to him who knocks it will be opened. Matthew 7:7-8 NKJV

Mrs. Lakeisha Osborne-Cannon is a Minister, conference speaker, preacher, mentor, entrepreneur, and owner of a Christian Montessori School. Having matriculated at Kean University, Pneuma Life School of Ministry, and Concordia University, obtaining a Bachelor's in Sociology, a master's in public administration, and soon a Doctorate in Leadership, Lakeisha is not only a voice to the Kingdom of God but also a voice to the millennial generation.

Kingdom Assignment

Ms. Lakeisha Osborne founded Thy Women of Royalty Ministries, Inc. As the CEO of WORTHY Ministries International and Thy Women of Royalty Ministries, she has established ministries such as the Worthy Girl School of Excellence, Inc., an organization focused on mentoring young girls.

Beverly A. Sylvester

PRAISE GOD DAILY
> I will bless the LORD at all times: His praise shall continually be in my mouth. Psalm 34:1

Praising God is offering up our hearts, minds, and spirits continually every day for all the wonderful things He has done, is doing, and is going to do in our lives. Upon waking, before your feet hit the floor in the morning, praise Him! When you feel like you need a "pick-me-up" in the afternoon, don't run for that second cup of coffee, offer up a praise! Remember to praise God throughout the day, even during the difficult times at home, work, or school, because praise is comely for God's people. (Psalm 33:1)

SEEK GOD FERVENTLY
> Seek the LORD while He may be found; call upon Him while He is near. Isaiah 55:6

God desires for us to seek Him with our whole heart. He wants an intimate relationship with His children. We are to make every effort to live in accordance with His holy word. And if we seek Him daily, preferably, before we start our day, then our directions, decisions, and wisdom needed will come! Listen, if we lost something that we deem very valuable, like money, a diamond ring, or credit cards, we would turn over tables searching for them. We'd skip a meal, not answer a phone call, or not turn on the TV to find that valuable "thing." Therefore, how much more important is it to seek God and His presence? So, today, make a conscious decision to seek the Lord with all of your heart. (Psalm 105:4)

WORSHIP GOD TRUTHFULLY

> God is a Spirit, and those who worship Him must worship in spirit and in truth. John 4:24

When I think of worship, I imagine the posture of prayer, bowing down on my knees in full surrender to my Lord and Savior Jesus Christ. A heart of worship is a heart that responds by acknowledging who God truly is. He is LORD, Sovereign, Creator, Redeemer, Protector, Provider, Comforter, Counselor, Friend, and the list goes on. In the dictionary, the word "Worship" is said to be "the feeling or expression of reverence and adoration for a deity." Let's remember, we worship and adore the one true and living God who created the heavens and the earth, formed man from the dust of the ground, loved us enough to send His Son to die that we might be saved from a life of sin, and who is coming back to take us to our eternal home to live with Him forever! Hallelujah!

TRUST GOD FAITHFULLY

> Blessed is the man who trusts in the LORD, and whose hope is the LORD. Jeremiah 17:7

Do we really trust God? Are we willing to open ourselves up and risk being vulnerable and naked before God? Are we willing to acknowledge Him in everything? I mean in EVERYTHING. That's what it means to trust God! Acknowledging Him in all our ways, not just in the easy and good times, but also in the hard places of our lives, when we cannot trace Him. Trust God because He has your back. Trust God because He knows what's best, and He gives only the best for His children. So, let's put our confidence in the only one who knows all things, has all power to change all things, and has wisdom in everything! (Proverbs 3:5,6)

THANK GOD ALWAYS

> Oh, give thanks unto the God of heaven! For His mercy endures forever. Psalm 136: 26

This should come naturally for every believer in Christ Jesus. However, I believe we fall short of this practice. In other words, we need to express our gratitude to God intentionally because we have so much to thank God for. When we wake up in the morning, be quick to thank Him for another day. Thank Him for the new mercies that He gives daily. Thank Him for family and friends. Thank Him for His holy word. Thank Him in every situation you find yourself in. And in everything give thanks, for this is the will of God in Christ Jesus concerning you. (1 Thessalonians 5:18)

I invite you to make this beautiful hymnal a sacred devotion to **GOD,** our heavenly Father:

> "Great is Thy faithfulness, O God my Father;
> There is no shadow of turning with Thee.
> Thou changest not, thy compassions, they fail not.
> As Thou hast been, thou forever will be.
>
> Great is Thy faithfulness,
> Great is Thy faithfulness,
> Morning by morning new mercies I see.
> All I have needed Thy hand hast provided;
> Great is Thy faithfulness, Lord unto me."

I am a wife, a mother of four, and a happy grandmother to a precious little girl. My family is my first priority in ministry. I grew up in a large family in Rochester, New York, as the 8th child out of 11. I was raised in a Christian home where we regularly attended church, prayer meetings, and revivals. At an early age, I accepted Jesus Christ as my personal Lord and Savior. After years of serving at the House of Prayer, Encouragement, and Empowerment ministry (HOPE), I was ordained in 2018 under the leadership of Pastor Marc S. Bryant. Through this ministry and the Global Compass Prayer Ministry (GCPM), my faith has deepened, and my love relationship with the Lord and His people has matured in many ways. My heart's desire is to continue growing closer to God, studying His word, serving my family, and touching many lives with the love of Jesus, both near and far.

Your Prayers Are Heard

Dr. Carla Palin

> O thou that hearest prayer, unto thee shall all flesh come. Psalm 65

The late Bishop Kenneth Flowers said, "The Lord hearing us is equivalent to Him answering us."

One of the most common questions we ask is, "Does God truly hear us? And why should we pray when He already knows what we need?" Dr. Myles Monroe offers a profound perspective: "Prayer is not just an activity, a ritual, or an obligation. It is communion and communication that touches God's Heart."

This Psalm is called a Psalm of Thanksgiving, which expresses public thanksgiving for what God has done or anticipation of what He will do. These Psalms offer comfort, encouragement, and blessing to God's people. It also praises God for His kindness and answers to prayer.

Answered prayer occurs when someone prays and receives what they prayed for. God always listens to us when we pray. The scriptures give us many examples of prayers the Father has heard and answered. In John 11, verses 41 and 42, Jesus is praying for Lazarus. He says, "Father, I thank thee that thou hast heard me, and I know that thou hearest me always. "Jesus was confident that when He called on the Father, the Father responded. Matthew 21:22 says, And all things, whatsoever ye shall ask in prayer, believing, ye shall receive. The key to answered prayer is to believe. Mark 11:22 – "Therefore, I say unto you, What things soever ye desire when ye pray, believe that ye receive them, and ye shall have them. Jesus has given us an open invitation to come to Him through prayer." Invitation to prayer allows us to connect with the Father and grow intimately with Him.

As we establish our relationship with the Father, we will know that He is the God who hears and answers prayers. Scripture shows us that God hears our requests and that He will answer them. 1 John 5:14-15 says, And this is the confidence that we have in him, that, if we ask anything according to His will, He heareth us. And if we know that He hears us whatsoever we ask, we know that we have the petition we desire of Him.

The second part of this verse in the Psalm says, "unto thee shall all flesh come." Some people hesitate to pray because they may not receive the desired answers. Some decide not to pray because our Father already knows what we want and need. Just like with our natural parents, as children when we wanted something, we had to ask. It is essential to bring your requests to God in prayer.

Elijah might have prayed on Mount Carmel with all the fire and energy of his soul, but no answer to his prayer has been given, and no glory would come to God. Peter might have shut himself up with Dorcas' dead body until her body came alive, but if no answer had come, no glory to God, not good to man, would have followed him. To answer to prayer is the part of prayer that glorifies God. (E.M. Bounds on Prayer - Answered Prayer)

Prayer is not merely a means of reaching out to God in times of need; it is a continuous line of communication through which we can hear from our Father. Understanding prayer's significance as a lifeline, we recognize that we cannot exist without it. Prayer's purpose is to convey the blessings God intends to bestow upon us. It serves as the divinely ordained channel through which all temporal and spiritual requests are fulfilled. Prayer is not an end in itself but brings peace and joy from the Father. Its ultimate goal is to secure an answer.

Just as God has commanded us to pray always, everywhere, and in everything, He promises to answer always, everywhere, and in everything.

> *Father, Your Word declares, "You are the Lord that hears and answers prayer, and unto you shall all flesh come." So, we pray for my brother and sisters in Jesus' name. I pray that they will come to you in confidence, knowing you are the Lord who awaits to hear our prayer. Father, thank You that Your ears are attentive to our cry. So, we call unto You today and pray that You will strengthen our faith and confidence in You. That whatsoever we desire, according to Your will, it will be granted to us. So, we thank You for hearing and answering us. We thank you for the privilege of calling You our Father. Thanks for granting us access to pray and watch you move on our behalf. For this is the confidence we have in You. We don't look to another, only you. We pray this prayer in Jesus' Name.*

> O thou that hearest prayer, unto thee shall all flesh come. Psalms 65:2

1. John 11:41 & 42 - Matthew 21:22 - Mark 11:22 - 1 John 5:14-15 (King James Version)
2. Power and Purpose of Prayer - Dr. Myles Monroe
3. Elijah Mount Carmel - 1 Kings 18:17-46
4. Dorcas - Acts 9:35-43
5. E.M. Bounds on Prayer - Answered Prayer – pg. 240

Dr. Carla Palin is a woman of faith and prayer and a prophet to the nations. Over 40 years ago, she answered the call to the ministry, a journey that has enriched her spiritual insights and teachings.

Dr. Palin holds a doctorate in Theology and a bachelor's degree in ministry leadership and is a Certified Life Coach. She is a dedicated leader who helps Pastors enhance their ministries through guidance, support, and prayer. As an entrepreneur, she founded two non-profits and is the founder of Dr. Carla Palin Ministries in Roselle, New Jersey.

Dr. Palin may be reached at drcarlapalinmin@outlook.com

Bold Prayer

Dr. Tricia Robinson

Do you have a dream that has died, or a desire that you thought, "Surely that will not happen in my life?" Can you remember a time when a verse struck your heart and you wondered what it really meant, or a time when you heard it, but then thought, "That verse surely does not apply to me?" There is something profound about reading and hearing God's word and being so in awe of the depth of its meaning. I recall being in the middle of a church service one Sunday morning when I heard part of a verse, "abundantly far more," or "exceedingly abundantly above" (New King James Version), and believing that it might be applicable to certain parts of my life, but not others. There is a tension within all of us where belief and unbelief can reside. In a similar vein as the man who approached Jesus and said, "I believe; help my unbelief" (Mark 9:25 NRSV), we should utter the same prayer, especially when met with his bold, amazing promises.

In what area of your life are you thinking that God cannot do exceedingly abundantly above what you could imagine? Does God lie? Can you reflect today on a specific scripture that attests to God's promise that He will surely bring His Word to pass?

The veil has been torn as we read in the book of Hebrews, and we can "boldly" come before the throne of grace. If only we were bold in our prayer life, then indeed more mountains would move. Did Jesus not say that if only we have faith as small as a mustard seed, then we could speak to the mountain in our life? It is through His power at work in us as believers that something amazing beyond our prayers, thoughts, or even feelings can be accomplished. That power comes from His Spirit moving in us. Allow that Spirit to fill your heart now. This verse from Ephesians dares us to ask for more from God and to have a vision for His kingdom. And that glory belongs to Him, because He can accomplish unbelievable things in our lives and in that of others as we intercede for them.

As we look at the context of this verse in Ephesians 3, we see Paul writing to encourage the hearts of other believers as he was suffering. He was praying that they did not lose heart (Eph 3:13). We know that Paul was interceding for the believers by his posture, which was that of bowing before the Father. Are we not to imitate those great saints who have gone before us? This means that we too are called to intercede for others even in the midst of our own deep and personal sufferings. God hears the prayers of those who suffer as Christ did, and even Christ pleaded in the garden before He went to the cross. We have a model of intercession and one that demonstrates that God can accomplish far more than our minds can comprehend. The disciples stood by the cross and yet did not understand what God accomplished in that moment. As they stood by the cross, their dreams and visions of the kingdom they thought Jesus would bring died. And yet, did not the true kingdom get revealed by the Lord's death? Our dear Savior interceded for His disciples before going to the cross, and God's name was glorified. His name continues to be glorified in His church and continues to achieve more for generations to come and forever. Jesus, the Alpha and Omega, the author and perfecter of our faith.

Though that time years ago in my life revealed the unbelief in my heart, God was gracious and patient with me and the unbelief was routed out. Now I have an additional testimony for what I have seen Him accomplish in that particular area of my life that I thought for sure was dead. How amazing is God! Believe in His promise today for your heart, and if your heart is hardened in any way, cry, "Help my unbelief." God desires to do bold things in your life and for your life to bring glory to His kingdom today. Allow His power to move in you today as you pray.

> Now to him who by the power at work within us is able to accomplish abundantly far more than all we can ask or imagine, to him be glory in the church and in Christ Jesus to all generations, forever, and ever. Amen. Ephesians 3:20 (New Revised Standard Version)

Dr. Tricia Robinson is a licensed clinical psychologist who is also board-certified in clinical psychology. She obtained her doctoral degree at George Washington University and her master's degree in counseling psychology from Gordon-Conwell Theological Seminary in 2000. She is passionate about empowering others for change and healing from their brokenness. You can contact her at contact@acumenpsychological.com.

Don't Doubt God

Dr. Veronica M. Ambrose

Doubt is one of the greatest enemies and obstacles of our faith. It slithers through cracks of uncertainty and during moments when we face circumstances that challenge us, doubt acts like a thief to steal our dreams, kill our destiny, and destroy our purpose by whispering lies that challenge God's promises. As believers, we must trust in God's unchanging nature and His unfailing word. We are called to reject doubt.

To doubt God is to limit Him and minimize His power. When we focus on the size of our problems more than the greatness of God, we risk diminishing our faith. Many figures in the Bible didn't focus on their physical limitations or on the problems. They did not care about being persecuted for standing on what they believed; they focused on the One who made the promise. This focus is important for us as believers. God's promises do not depend on our strength or circumstances; they are grounded in His immutability. Doubt arises when we measure God by human standards, but faith grows when we measure our problems by God's infinite power. He is omnipotent. Don't doubt God.

It is vital to our Christian journey to honor God by not doubting Him. Ultimately trusting God opens doors to a life of divine favor, peace, joy, and fruitfulness. Refusing to doubt God, and trusting Him in everything we do, we can live without worry, anxiety, fear, or stress. We need God all the time. We must lean on Him at all times and in all things. The word of God tells us in **Prov. 3:5-6:**

> Trust in the Lord with all your heart; do not depend on your own understanding. Seek His will in all you do, and He will show you which path to take. (NLT)

No situation is too small or too big for God. We have a covenant with God.

Abraham's unwavering and unswaggering faith is a blueprint for overcoming doubt and holding fast to God's promises. His story began with a promise: God promised Him descendants as numerous as the stars **(Genesis 15:5)**. Yet, Abraham and Sarah were childless, and time was against them, as they were old and past child-bearing age.

Like Abraham, we've received promises from God, but the waiting season tests our faith. Doubt often arises when there's a period between the promise and its fulfillment, but God's timing is perfect. **Isaiah 40:31** reminds us, **"They that wait upon the Lord shall renew their strength."** Don't let the waiting season rob you of your confidence in God. Instead, use it to refine and strengthen your trust. Abraham remained convinced that God would do as He said. While waiting, God often works on our character, preparing us for the blessing. Trusting God and holding on to His promises requires patience and total surrender, knowing that His promises may not come when we expect but knowing they will always come at the right time. Use the waiting season to deepen your relationship with God through prayer, fasting, and studying the word to build your spiritual stamina.

Romans 4:20 tells us, **"He did not waver through unbelief."** Abraham chose faith despite his physical and emotional limitations. His body was old, Sarah's womb was barren, yet he believed. Having faith does not mean the absence of doubt but it is refusing to let doubt dictate your decisions. In fact, the scripture says that Abraham was "strengthened in his faith," demonstrating that faith is about growing stronger and developing spiritual muscles in the process. Every time we choose to use our measure of faith over doubt, we grow spiritually, emotionally, mentally, and become more confident in who we are in Christ.

Abraham "gave glory to God" even before seeing the fulfillment of the promise which exemplified faith. Praising God before the promise came to pass was rooted in who God is. This act of worship demonstrates the essence of true faith. When we trust God without doubting, our faith becomes a testimony to others, providing encouragement to those who are struggling, and glorifying God. Like Abraham, our confidence in God should be so steadfast that it becomes a source of encouragement for others, pointing them to His faithfulness. Abraham's faith gave Him the ability to glorify God even before the promise was fulfilled. This shows us that worship and trust go hand in hand. When we trust God fully, we can praise Him with confidence, knowing that He will fulfill His word.

Reflect on God's track record. Abraham remembered God's faithfulness in past experiences, and it fueled his trust in God's promise. When we face trials, it is important to look back on what God has already done in your lives. Has He ever failed you? The same God who delivered you yesterday is still working today. He protected Daniel in the lion's den, and He is your protector; don't doubt God! When Shadrach, Meshach, and Abednego were placed in the fire, He stepped in as the fourth man and kept them so that not even one hair on their head was burned, they did not even smell like smoke. No matter how hot the "fire" is on your spiritual journey, He will step in right-on-time and shield you. When you trust God, you will not look nor smell like what you have been through. He parted the Red Sea. So, whatever your red sea is He will do the same for you. He raised Jairus's daughter. What is dead in your life? God can bring it back to life!

Verse 21 declares that Abraham was **"fully persuaded that God had power to do what He had promised."** What Does It Mean to

Be Fully Persuaded? It means trusting God even when the outcome is unseen. It is believing that God's ability is greater than any obstacle. This is not based on our ability or circumstances but on God's unchanging nature. Numbers 23:19 reminds us that God is not a man that He should lie. If He said it, it will surely come to pass. Abraham's story is proof that God honors faith. Even when the timeline doesn't align with our expectations, we can rest in the assurance that His timing is perfect, and His promises are sure.

God's Word doesn't instantly erase all of life's challenges, but it provides strength, guidance, and the hope we need to navigate through them immediately. Christians still face the same troubles as anyone else. John 16:33 tells us, "I have told you all this so that you may have peace in me. Here on earth, you will have many trials and sorrows. But take heart because I have overcome the world." But what God does is He provides hope to sustain us. God is aware of all that you are going through. He is omniscient-He knows all things. He not only knows but He is working on your behalf for good. No matter how dark your situation is, He will keep you whose mind is stayed on Him. If you are stuck in a deep pit, God will send a lifeline to sustain you while you wait on your breakthrough. Don't doubt God! He is an on-time God! He is Jehovah Jireh, our God who shall supply all our needs. When the day comes for your victory, praise Him.

The life of Abraham serves as a powerful reminder to never doubt God. Refuse to focus on the impossibilities and choose to magnify the God who specializes in the impossible. Romans 4:20-21 challenges us to be "fully convinced" that God is able to do all He has promised. When doubt tries to creep in, let us remember His faithfulness in the past and the countless testimonies of others who trusted Him. As you trust Him, your faith will grow stronger, your hope will be renewed, and you will see His promises fulfilled. Do not doubt God, for He is faithful, able, and always on time.

Trust Him, for God's promises are sure, and His power is limitless. He will do what He has promised! So, let us stand firm in faith, glorify Him, and remain confident that what He has spoken, He will bring to pass. Do not doubt God, for He is faithful and able!

> Abraham never wavered in believing God's promise. In fact, his faith grew stronger, and in this he brought glory to God. He was fully convinced that God is able to do whatever he promises. Romans 4:20-21(NLT)

Dr. Veronica M. Ambrose is an esteemed educator and spiritual leader. She serves as Pastor and President of the Women's Ministry at Abundant Grace Worship Ministries. She works as an educator at Battle Hill Elementary School in New Jersey while holding the position of Vice President at Grace Hill Bible University. Her academic credentials include degrees from Sam Sharpe Teachers' College, a bachelor's degree from Kean University, a master's degree from Walden University, and an associate, bachelor's, master's, doctorate, and PhD from Grace Hill Bible University. Dr. Ambrose has positively impacted her community through mentorship, educational programs, and support for people experiencing homelessness. She embodies faith and service, focusing on providing educational resources to underprivileged children. You can contact her at drvambrose@gmail.com.

Watch and Pray in Faith

Reverend Adrianne Smiling

Why watch and pray? Why pray in faith? Why? Prayer is our connection with God, our Father. When we open our hearts and minds to communicate with Father God, He is prepared to consider our prayer petition. God is more than able to manage the burdens of this world, daily concerns, and issues. We do not know what tomorrow holds; however, we do know who holds our tomorrow. Develop a rapport with the Father. One of the characteristics of God the Father is omniscience; He knows all, and nothing surprises Him. We can watch with our natural eyes and see things from one perspective; however, when we watch with a spiritual or supernatural sense, the view gains clarity.

God will guide you when you communicate with Him. We know our parents, and our parents know us because of our relationship with them. As parents, we often sense when our children need to communicate with us. We pray in faith because, as the word says, how much more will God give us the good things we request that are in His will.

The posture of prayer is important. God is Holy, and when we pray, our posture should begin with humility and thankfulness. Acknowledge God's power and gratefulness. Pray in faith, knowing there is nothing too hard for God to accomplish. He is the Great I Am. Faith is a form of trust, and trust is developed through relationships. The threads of prayer are woven with people, places, situations, events, and desires presented to the throne of God and Jesus Christ, our Intercessor.

There is power in the petitions of the righteous praying in faith for the favor of God. Develop and maintain a connection and communication with your prayer life. Increase your faith in prayer; this is profitable for your spiritual growth and maturity. Why not pray to the Father who has all power and loves you? How do you know that God loves you? He gave His *only* Son to stand on your behalf and take on your sins. He loves us so much that we are created in His image and likeness (Genesis 1:27). He is patient and kind. He hears us.

Call to God, and the Lord saves you (Psalms 55:16). Become childlike in your relationship with the Almighty, humble yourself, and open up to God with deliberate communication; pray. Strengthen your relationship with God the Father, God the Son, and God the Holy Spirit. Communicate with Him.

> Devote yourselves to prayer, being watchful and thankful. Colossians 4:2 NIV

Reverend Adrianne Smiling and her husband, Mr. Smiling, have been married for 37 years and reside in Somerset County, NJ. The Smilings have reared their family according to Joshua 24:15: "But as for me and my household, we will serve the LORD." Rev. Smiling has served as an Intercessor with the Global Compass Prayer Ministry since 2013 and is a member of the Executive Committee, to aid in the facilitation of the vision of the leadership through fervent prayers. She is an ordained minister, intercessor, retiree, wife, mother of two daughters, one son-in-love, and one granddaughter. In October 2023, Rev. Smiling and her husband launched True Vine Family Ministry online. She has made a significant impact on the youth, mentoring girls and sharing her passion for prayer. The ministry emphasizes the hope of generational blessings, peace, truth, prosperity, and purpose while praying for all youth and children. Recently, the ministry published "Prayer for the Schools" on the ministry's YouTube channel to encourage saturating children and schools with effective, fervent prayers. Reverend Smiling can be contacted via email at rev.asmiling35@gmail.com, and content can be viewed on YouTube under True Vine Family Ministry.

Victory Over Trials and Tribulations

Elder Crystal R. Steward

In this life, we will be faced with trials and tribulations. The word of God declares in John 16:33, "These things I have spoken unto you, that in me ye might have peace. In the world ye shall have tribulation: but be of good cheer; I have overcome the world." We can be assured that even though there are tribulations in this world, we have overcome this world because Jesus has made us a victorious people. If we believe in Jesus Christ, we overcome this world and we are victorious.

> For whatsoever is born of God overcometh the world: and this is the victory that overcometh the world, even our faith. Who is he that overcometh the world, but he that believeth that Jesus is the Son of God?
> 1 John 5:4

We have faith in the word of God and know that we have victory in the midst of every circumstance that we are confronted with. We must continue to encourage ourselves in the word of God. Trials and tribulations come to make us strong. We know if God delivered us before, He can do it again and again. We are built up on our most holy faith. Faith that no matter what we experience and go through God will always bring us through. He will never fail us and is mighty to deliver us right in the midst of the trial. He is able to bring us through it if we look to Jesus as the author and finisher of our faith.

The enemy brings trials and tribulations to discourage us from keeping the faith. He walks around like a roaring lion, and all he has to do is growl, and we will tuck our tail like a scared puppy and run. 1 Peter 5:8 says, "Be sober, be vigilant; because your adversary the devil, as a roaring lion, walketh about, seeking whom he may devour." The devil is not a lion; he just tries to imitate one. He does come to steal, kill, and destroy. Jesus came that we might have life and that more abundantly. We do not have to surrender to the tricks and schemes of Satan when he brings trials and tribulations. We put our trust in a never-lose God that is able to bring us out of every horrible pit.

Tribulations and trials come to hinder us and discourage us in our walk with Jesus. Tribulations will increase our faith and trust in the almighty God and the perfect finished work of Jesus Christ, who gave his life for us. We have access to faith by his grace.

> And not only so, but we glory in tribulations also: knowing that tribulation worketh patience; 5:4 And patience, experience; and experience, hope: 5:5 And hope maketh not ashamed; because the love of God is shed abroad in our hearts by the Holy Ghost which is given unto us. Romans 5:3

We gain patience through tribulations because we have to wait and trust God to move on our behalf. We know through experience that God will bring us through trials and tribulations because he did it before. Waiting and having patience for God to deliver us brought about experience. Experience produced trust and hope to know without any doubt that Jesus would deliver us. We know that because of our hope in the all-seeing, all-knowing

God and the victory of Jesus, we will not be made ashamed. Trials and tribulations will help us to know that we are overcomers; no matter what we might go through, we can shout it out from the rooftop, "I'm coming out!" We can glory and rejoice in tribulations and trials. The word sums it up this way: 2 Corinthians 4:8 "We are troubled on every side, yet not distressed; we are perplexed, but not in despair; 4:9 Persecuted, but not forsaken; cast down, but not destroyed; 4:10 Always bearing about in the body the dying of the Lord Jesus, that the life also of Jesus might be made manifest in our body."

During trials and tribulations, we must pray. We should pray without ceasing, knowing that we are communicating with God and Jesus who sits at the right hand of the Father, making intercession for us. I am reminded of an old familiar hymn that is able to clarify our need for prayer during trials and tribulations.

What a friend we have in Jesus
All our sins and griefs to bear
What a privilege to carry
Everything to God in prayer
Oh, what peace we often forfeit
Oh, what needless pain we bear
All because we do not carry
Everything to God in prayer
Have we trials and temptations?
Is there trouble anywhere?
We should never be discouraged
Take it to the Lord in prayer
Can we find a friend so faithful
Who will all our sorrows share?
Jesus knows our every weakness
Take it to the Lord in prayer

So, we must take everything we are faced with to God in prayer. Jesus will hear us when we pray and make a way out of no way. We will experience good success if we pray according to the word of God. We will face trials and tribulations, but we will come through them by trusting God and relying on Him to deliver us through Jesus, who conquered death, hell, and the grave so that we might be victorious.

Elder Crystal R. Steward was born in Winter Park, Florida, where she currently resides. She is a retired educator and serves as an ordained Elder, Teacher, and Prophetic Psalmist in her local church. She believes it is essential as a part of the Five-fold Ministry to perfect the saints.

Prayer Changes Things

Global Compass
Prayer Ministries Inc.

If it Wasn't True, He Would Have Told Me

Stephanie Torrey

Little did I know, in the early days of my Christian walk, I would utter what would soon become prophetic to my husband: "Our faith hasn't really been tested."

Up until then, my faith journey was uneventful and joyful. Our family cherished the love, warmth, and fellowship of our church community. However, that peaceful existence came to a halt one fateful Saturday night in 2009, when our four-year-old daughter, Rachel, suddenly became unresponsive.

The one thing that will test any marriage is when your children's health is at stake.

I had gone into our bedroom and saw our daughter sitting motionless on my husband's lap while he was watching TV, her gaze fixed on the ceiling.

"Do you see angels?" I asked, unaware that in a matter of moments, we would be fervently praying and calling upon the Lord and His angels. When our daughter remained unresponsive to both my husband and me, I immediately dialed 911. Without a moment's hesitation, and without even pausing to put on his shoes, my husband rushed our daughter to the car and sped towards the hospital.

James told us when trials come, to count it as joy (James 1:2), however, all I could feel in that moment was panic. Yet, somehow, even in the midst of my panic, by the grace of God, I tried to focus and hold onto my faith.

My 11-year-old son, William, was visibly upset as we prepared to meet my husband and daughter at the hospital. In what now seems like a small act of faith, I stopped and calmly reminded my son, "This is when we need to trust God."

I had dared to believe in the midst of this situation to trust Jesus. My heart racing and trembling, I held fast to who I knew God to be: faithful. He's faithful even when we are faithless.

Jesus told His disciples in John 14:1-2, "Let not your heart be troubled." The same holds true for us as Christ followers. He said to them, and He's saying to His sons and daughters today: don't let your heart trouble you because of the problems. "You believe in God, believe also in Me."

Why would the Lord tell us this? Because it's true. If it wasn't true, He would have told us.

I mean, surely at this point, His disciples had seen Jesus do it all. They knew that He was God. He couldn't fail. But yet and still, Jesus had to reassure and remind them that if they believed in God, then they can and should believe Him.

Certainly, we too have seen and experienced God's faithfulness time and again when our backs were against the wall. But, like the disciples, we forget, and we doubt.

When we go through seasons that test our faith, the Lord does not want our hearts to be troubled and dismayed. Our hearts are deceitful, and our emotions will lead us astray in those moments of testing. But Jesus is bigger than our emotions and bigger than our moments. We can take God at His Word and believe Him.

During our times of adversity, it's hard to see the forest for the trees. It's difficult to see the Lord's wonderful plan and purpose. But it's important to look for Jesus.

Even though I couldn't comprehend what was happening with our daughter, I knew prayer and trust in God were my only recourse. God's presence was evident in the support of our church family, who walked alongside us through this trial.

As it turned out, my daughter had a seizure. This would be something she would contend with in her early childhood years. During that time, we faced some hard challenges, but God!

The Lord eventually healed our daughter, in His time.

My faith in Christ also deepened. The faith of our family continued to be tested through our son's health struggles, which started from his teens and extended into college.

Nevertheless, the Lord was faithful throughout it all. And that which the Enemy had meant for evil against my family, specifically our children, God turned it around for good!

If it wasn't true, He would have told me.

> Let not your heart be troubled; you believe in God, believe also in Me. In My Father's house are many mansions; if it were not so, I would have told you.
> John 14:1-2

Stephanie Torrey wears many hats as a devotional writer, speaker, prayer leader, and minister.

She encourages others through her writings on her blog, "Speaking Truth In Love" (speakingtruthinlov.com), where she shares messages of faith, truth, and love with an emphasis on Scripture. Stephanie's passion for encouraging others extends to her work as a speaker and prayer leader with Global Compass Prayer Ministry. She also brings her dedication to faith in her role as a minister at The HOPE.

You can find her on Facebook: facebook.com/speakingtruthinlov, Instagram: speakingtruthinlov.

My Source

Diana Treadwell

> I will say of the Lord, He is my refuge and fortress, my God, in whom I trust. Psalm 91

Source is defined as a place, person, or thing from which something comes or can be obtained.

For those who love the Lord, Jesus is the Source!!! We cannot do anything without HIM. No matter what we do, we cannot do anything apart from Him - NOTHING without the SOURCE! God is the husbandman, our source! John 15:1. God will cut off and cut out the things in your life that bear no fruit (those things that hinder you from being a better person).

> I will not leave you or forsake you. John 15: 2 – 6

When God prunes you and purges you, it may not feel good, but it is for your good and gives you the ability to look more like Jesus. When God purges you, the Holy Spirit cleanses you of sin and delivers you from dead works. God will give you power to produce good fruit through the Spirit because He knows what's in you. God will never forget about you, even if you become disconnected. He said He will be with you always (Psalm 23:4). He will fulfill His promise to never leave you or forsake you. Stay in alignment with God's word. We have to stay connected to the source – the Word of God!

Philippians 4:6-7 says, "by prayer and supplication with thanksgiving let your requests be made known to God." Hebrews 13:6 says, "The Lord is my helper; I will not fear." Genesis 28:15 says, "Behold, I am with you and will keep you wherever you go, for I will not leave you until I have done what I have promised you."

Obedience began at the cross when Jesus bled and died for our sakes (Deuteronomy 31:6,8, Matt 28:20). We should thank Jesus daily for being obedient until death and being the source of our existence.

> *Order our steps today, Jesus. Thank you, Lord, for moving in the situations in our hearts and minds.*

Abide in the Lord, and the Lord will abide in you. Let us bear good fruit through the Spirit. Stay connected to the source—God; He chose you. Have a safe and wonderful day.

> *Father, thank You for being our source, the One in whom we can depend. Help us to stay connected to You in every situation. We pray for your guidance and strength. Help us to not be moved by circumstances or situations that are beyond our control. We know You are our source, our strength, and You have everything under control. Help us to continually keep our eyes on You and not our circumstances because we know You love us and desire that we prosper and be in good health. So, we trust You and honor You. Amen, amen, and amen.*

Minister Diana Treadwell is the co-founder of Global Compass Prayer Ministries. She is a member of a 50 and Older prayer group, and she partners and prays with other prayer groups and teams around the country. Even though she has been dealing with various health problems, she relies on her SOURCE. She has a heart and a passion for the Lord and shares her passion whenever possible.

Growing in Love

Jannie Broxton

> Dear friends, let us love one another, for love comes from God. Everyone who loves has been born of God and knows God. I John 4:7

Jesus says that it is by our love towards others that people will know that we are His disciples (John 13:35). I first received Christ in college, and my behavior did not reflect a Christian. I was awful. I prayed the prayers of an immature Christian, which were based on what I wanted and desired. My life was self-absorbed, which was reflected in my relationships.

I had a dear friend who helped me through college, and I rewarded him with a cold heart. I was so ashamed of my behavior that I forced myself not to think about it. God, being God, gave me another opportunity after I joined the military to reconcile with him, but I would not acknowledge that I knew him, and I walked right past him. My behavior was rude, selfish, and prideful, which is the opposite of what Christ taught.

Unfortunately, he is deceased, and I will never have another opportunity to apologize for my ungodly behavior. What do you do when God's word says to love everyone, and you fail? I prayed for forgiveness, and I repented of my sins, asking God to create in me a clean heart and renew a right spirit within me.

Love for God and others is the foundation of Christianity. God is love and whoever lives in love lives in God, and God in them (I John 4:16). The gift of love that we receive from the Holy Spirit is called agape love. Agape love is one of the fruits of the Spirit, and as with any gift, it has to be received and cultivated.

Let's discuss the different types of love:
- Eros love - it refers to erotic love - sexual love.
- Storge love - it refers to family love, the kind of love there is between a parent and child, or between family members in general.
- Philia love - it's brotherly friendship and affection. It is the love of deep friendship and partnership. It is described as the highest love that one is capable of without God's help.

Agape love - a love that loves without changing. It is a self-giving love that gives without demanding or expecting repayment. It is love so great that it can be given to the unlovable or unappealing. It is love that loves even when it is rejected. It does not love to receive. This type of love is only possible when you are a child of God, and He is working a new life within you. Agape love is indescribable to those who don't know the love of Jesus. (by Barbara Sande-Heavenonwheels).

Eros, storge and philia are natural love that are based on feelings and emotions with fleshly desires. Agape love is not natural love, it's spiritual and given by the Holy Spirit through prayer. It is a divine, supernatural love that is unconditional and sacrificial. Agape love was demonstrated by God, Jesus, Abraham, The Good Samaritans, and others in the Bible.

God demonstrated His love in John 3:16, which says: "God so loved the world that He gave His only begotten Son." I Peter 2:24 says: "Christ bore our sins in His body on the cross so that we might die to sin and live to righteousness." Genesis 22:9-10 discusses how Abraham offered his son to God as an offering. Luke 10:25-37 disclosed how the Good Samaritan gave his time, effort, and money to help a Jewish man who usually had no interactions with Samaritans. Each one of these have two things in common, they demonstrated agape love and each action was self-sacrificing.

In John 13:35b; Jesus states, "by love they will know that you are my disciples." Why? Disciples follow Jesus' commandments to love God and others, they pray, and they have an intimate relationship with Jesus Christ. John 15:9-10 9. "As the Father has loved me, so have I loved you. Now remain in my love. 10. If you keep my commands, you will remain in my love, just as I have kept my Father's commands and remain in his love.

Agape love is under the anointing of the Holy Spirit.

Romans 5:5 says: And hope does not put us to shame, because God's love has been poured out into our hearts through the Holy Spirit, who has been given to us. The love that we demonstrate to others brings people to Christ. Love is a precious gift; it heals, teaches, encourages, inspires, and grows within us and others, whether it is conscious or unconscious. When we extend a kind word or a helping hand to those who are down and out, it gives hope to others.

It is God's intention to show His love through us by any means possible.

Genuine love will humble you and allow the Holy Spirit to lead you into unselfish acts if you allow it. Have you ever given of yourself unselfishly? I Cor. 13:2-3 expresses the importance of agape love, it states: But if I have not love, I am nothing, and I gain nothing. If your motives for what you say and do are not based on love, then you've wasted your time.

Nothing will come of it.

There is a reason God placed love at the top of the hierarchy of gifts, because love is so powerful that it transforms people's hearts and minds to what is God's good, acceptable, and perfect will. Love strengthens Christians to not give up or give in until God's will is done in a specific situation.

It is God's intention to show His love through us.

As I prayed and matured in Christ, I was transformed into a person who loved God and others. I was no longer self-centered, but God-focused. Prayer changed me! And the Lord led me into numerous prayer ministries with a desire to pray for whom He places on my heart. Make no mistakes, agape love elevates us into a higher dimension in the things of God. It allows the Holy Spirit to lead us into the deeper things of God so that we are working with God and not just for Him. It is our love for God and others with prayer that unites and connects the Body of Christ.

Don't do what I have done by not taking advantage of an opportunity to apologize for ungodly behavior. God is a forgiving God and always gives us an opportunity to get it right, so get it right now!

Matthew 6:15 says: But if you do not forgive others their sins, your Father will not forgive your sins. Don't allow your opportunity to love and forgive another person pass you by. Choose love and forgiveness. Love is powerful, and it covers a multitude of sins (I Peter 4:8).

LET LOVE CHANGE YOU!!!!

Let us pray.

Almighty and powerful God, forgive me for my sins.

Lord, I ask that the Holy Spirit consume and permeate every area of my heart, mind, and soul, filling me with the gift of agape love. Jesus, heal what is broken within me, and I forgive all who have wronged me.

Jesus, I ask that you pour out your love through me into others.

In Jesus Christ's name! Amen!!!

Jannie Broxton, Registered Nurse, BSN, MA in Theology, and a Member of Greater Shiloh Church, is involved in the following Ministries: Deuteronomy Ministry (feeding the homeless), Global Compass Prayer Ministry, God Is Real Prayer Ministry, Freedom Prayer Ministry, and The 24 Hours Prayer Ministry.

Strength for the Journey

Elder Kim R. Hernandez

When my daughter was diagnosed with breast cancer, my world felt as though it had been turned upside down. As a mother, nothing could have prepared me for the mix of emotions I felt fear, helplessness, anger, and deep sorrow. Yet, in that moment of overwhelming uncertainty, I felt a quiet prompting – a reminder that I didn't have to face this battle alone. God was with us.

I remembered the words from Isaiah 41:10, "So do not fear, for I am with you; do not be dismayed, for I am your God. I will strengthen you and help you; I will uphold you with my righteous right hand." This verse became a lifeline; a promise I clung to every day. When fear would creep in, I would remind myself that God was not only walking beside us but that He was also holding us up when we didn't have the strength to stand.

Through countless doctor's visits she attended and tearful prayers, I learned to surrender my worry to God in a way I had never done before. I leaned on Him for wisdom in navigating her care, for comfort in moments of despair, and for the courage to be her strength when she was weak. Day by day, I saw God's faithfulness shine through in small ways—a comforting word from a friend, a good report from the doctor, even just the strength to smile when everything seemed dim.

Looking back, I see how this trial became a journey of deepened faith and trust in the One who sustains us. God took what felt impossible and used it to remind me of His power to hold us, to give us peace beyond understanding, and to carry us through the valleys. I may not understand why we had to go through this, but I am grateful for the way it revealed God's enduring love and faithfulness in our lives.

I found Strength in the Storm

In those early days, fear and worry tried to take root. But as I cried out to God, I found a surprising strength rising within me—a strength that was not my own. I clung to scriptures that reminded me of God's power to sustain us. Philippians 4:13 says, "I can do all things through Christ who strengthens me." This verse became my anthem, my reminder that even though my heart was heavy, I was not alone in carrying this burden. God was giving me the strength to face each day.

Isaiah 40:31 also became a source of comfort: "But those who hope in the Lord will renew their strength. They will soar on wings like eagles; they will run and not grow weary; they will walk and not be faint." Every time I felt weak or overwhelmed, I would return to this promise. God was not asking me to do this in my strength; He was asking me to lean into His. The power of this verse carried me through many tearful nights, renewing my spirit when I felt I had nothing left to give.

As my daughter navigated the hospital visits alone, treatments, and uncertainty in the midst of a pandemic was isolating and exhausting. The restrictions kept us from seeing loved ones who might have offered comfort, and the fear of illness added yet another layer of concern. Yet, even in those isolated moments, God drew close. I saw His presence in unexpected places—a kind nurse, a friend's text, or a gentle reminder from scripture that we are held in His hands.

Throughout this season, I experienced God as both my strength and my comforter. I learned to trust Him in deeper ways, finding that in every moment of weakness, His strength was enough. Even now, I'm grateful for how God carried us through the storm, sustaining us with a love and power that is truly beyond understanding. This reflection shows how God was a constant anchor even amidst the pandemic's added challenges. I found myself asking, "Lord, how will I endure this? How can I be strong for her when my own heart feels so broken?"

In those moments of deep vulnerability, God reminded me of His promise in 2 Corinthians 12:9: "My grace is sufficient for you, for my power is made perfect in weakness." I realized I didn't have to rely on my own strength to weather this storm. In my weakest moments, God's strength was made all the more evident. He invited me to lean on Him completely, to surrender the fight and trust that He would hold us both.

Psalm 46:1 also became a refuge for my heart: "God is our refuge and strength, an ever-present help in trouble." These words carried me through countless nights when fear would creep in, and I would worry about what tomorrow would hold. I saw that God was with us right there in the storm, not just as a distant protector but as an ever-present help, walking with us through every medical appointment, treatment, and uncertainty.

In times of prayer, I found myself releasing my fear into His hands and asking for His peace to fill me. And He did. It wasn't always an instant calm but a steady assurance that I was not alone. God was the anchor in this storm, holding me steady and strengthening me in ways I didn't think possible.

The journey wasn't easy, but it was through this trial that I experienced the depth of God's love and strength. He didn't remove the storm; He empowered me to face it with a peace that surpassed all understanding. Today, I am grateful for the resilience He gave me and the reminder that no matter how fierce the storm, God's strength is always enough to carry us through.

> So do not fear, for I am with you; do not be dismayed, for I am your God. Isaiah 41:10
>
> I can do all things through Christ who strengthens me. Philippians 4:13
>
> But those who wait on the LORD shall renew their strength; They shall mount up with wings like eagles, they shall run and not be weary, they shall walk and not faint. Isaiah 40:31

I leave you with this:

> Pray without ceasing, and stand; when you have done all you can, stand believing if He said it, He will do it. Faith is what moves the hand of God. Without faith, it is impossible to please God. Prayer is the greatest power God has given us; it's our superpower, infused by our daily communion through our relationship with almighty God. 1 Thessalonians 5:17

Elder Kim R. Hernandez has been a devoted intercessor for over 30 years, serving faithfully on the Intercession Prayer Team at The Love of Jesus Family Church. Ordained as an Elder in 2009, she continues to stand in the gap for others through prayer, believing in the power of intercession to transform lives. In addition, she has been a committed intercessor with Global Compass Prayer Ministry for over 10 years, expanding her reach in spiritual warfare and prophetic intercession.

Beyond ministry, Elder Kim has dedicated her career to mental health and counseling. With a bachelor's degree in Sociology/Psychology and a Master's in Mental Health Counseling, she has worked extensively with the mentally and behaviorally challenged population. Currently, she serves as a Student Assistance Counselor at Saint Thomas Aquinas High School, where she provides emotional, behavioral, and spiritual support to students, helping them navigate life's challenges with faith and resilience.

With a heart for both healing and empowerment, Elder Kim is passionate about integrating faith and counseling to bring restoration to individuals and communities. Her mission is to uplift, encourage, and guide others toward wholeness—spiritually, emotionally, and mentally.

Faith. Favor. Freedom

Michele B. Thompson

A lump! Oh no! In October 2023, I was on a mission to find answers to my thoughts and my pain. The thought was, 'I think I feel a lump.' The pain was in my left breast. Immediately, I was reminded that four years prior, my sister had died from breast cancer. I knew my mind could not stay there with that thought. Two months later, after many phone calls to doctors and appointments for images, the unthinkable diagnosis was revealed: breast cancer. The mission: knowing I'm already healed through faith, prayer, and trust in Our Lord.

My faith in the Lord reminded me that my sister's story is not my story. I shall live and not die. This sickness is not unto death. (John 11:4) Yes, even cancer. It was my faith that allowed me to see that I was already healed. The choices I made during my treatment were based on my faith and trust in the Lord. Was I afraid and faced with anxiety? Absolutely! But God. God is so gracious. So much is possible with God, even when you have faith as small as a mustard seed (Matthew 17:20). God, we thank you for Your love!

Which situation caused you to lean on your faith? What "oh no!" experience have you faced? Can you recall at least one? Has it caused you to think of how you're going to get through it? Prayer is what brought me through, and the fact that you are reading this is proof that you believe in the power of prayer, too.

Prayer is a lifestyle. Prayer has no ending. My prayer life started early on in life- over 30 years ago, in the days when churches had Friday night prayer meetings, I would pick up the seniors and take them. There, I learned that prayer is a conversation with the Lord. It's not always about asking Him for things, but it's giving Him thanks and praise. Prayer is not hard. It can be as simple as saying, "God, I thank You." Do you recall when and how you started your prayer life? Who's watching you pray? Do you know that many of us are still reaping the blessings of prayers sown by people who may no longer be in the land of the living?

The Bible says to pray without ceasing, and we ought to take that to heart. Prayer brings us through. Prayer has always been a lifestyle for me. Even still, my mind goes through different channels due to the diagnosis and various treatments. However, what I did not know was that my prayer partner of sixteen years would not be here with me during this season of my life. In sixteen years, to go from praying daily, not missing a day, to her not being here was very painful. Just imagine, she transitioned one month after I was diagnosed. We don't know the future. However, God does. Thankfully, before she transitioned, my prayer life with my prayer partner branched off to the Thursday Morning Live with Chief Prayer Warrior Dr. Tincie Lynch. She and I would wake up at 5 am each day and come together with Dr. Lynch and the other prayer warriors. Being connected with Dr. Lynch has allowed me to be connected with many more prayer warriors at noon on every Monday, Wednesday, and Friday. Prayer is truly a lifeline. It is the first thing that we do with each day that God blesses us with. If it is not already, make prayer your top priority and connect with others to do so.

I trust the Lord because of how He has brought me through so many trials and tribulations before; how this, too, He will bring me through. Yes, can I tell you what the Lord has done! All glory to God! I am healed of cancer, and I'm still trusting God for the things I had no idea would stem from the Goldilocks Double Mastectomy surgery. I trust you, Lord! Do you trust the Lord to bring you through?

> Trust in the Lord with all your heart and lean not on your own understanding. Proverbs 3:5

Don't try to understand why you are going through.

When I think about what the Lord has done for me, He truly kept me and set me free. Now, when I think, I think about how God brought me through this healing journey, and I give Him all the glory. I think about how I focused on Him and not it. I never said, "my cancer". I never owned it. I never spoke the cancer word. When I think about how God orchestrated much-needed vital support from my children, siblings, doctors, nurses, friends, prayer warriors abroad, church family, co-workers, and the chief navigators, My God, I thank you!

Oh, can I tell you, "when I think". It only takes a moment, just "think". Think of what the Lord has done for you. You don't have to think too far back. Just think, He woke you up. Just think about the times He provided the jobs, kept your mind, protected you and yours from seen and unseen danger, healed your body, delivered you, and didn't allow you to give up when you wanted to. Oh yes, just think. I know the list goes on. We owe Him much praise. Keep the faith, know that we are favored, and live in the freedom of knowing we shall keep going and live.

> O Lord my God, I cried out to You, And You healed me. Psalm 30:2

This is the day that the Lord has made; let us rejoice and be glad in it. Dear Heavenly Father, I come with thanksgiving in my heart. Thank You, Lord, for forgiving me of my sins. I come repenting as well.

Lord, I thank You for last night's slumber and for this morning's rising. Yesterday is gone, but You granted us another day with new beginnings, hope, peace, love, joy, and favor. Lord, thank You for being the God that You are. The God who cares, loves, heals, forgives, and meets us at our point of need. You are the God who never leaves us nor forsake us. You are the God with all power.

Lord, I thank You for being the healer that You are. You have the power to heal all manner of sickness and disease, even cancer. Lord, nothing is too hard for You,

Michele B. Thompson is a certified paralegal from Alexandria, Virginia. Michele's experience on the frontline tapped into one of her passions - taking care of and encouraging others. She is the founder of MBT Paralegal Services. To encourage your audience, invite her on your platform or podcasts by contacting her at 240.490.9446, michele@mbtparalegalservices.com, or finding her on Facebook at Faith Favor Freedom.

Look Up to God

Vernesa Penny Green

Numbers 21:5-9 exemplifies the themes of human discontent, the consequences of sin, the necessity of repentance, and the provision of healing and salvation.

> They traveled from Mount Hor along the route to the Red Sea, to go around Edom. But the people grew impatient on the way; they spoke against God and against Moses, and said, "Why have you brought us up out of Egypt to die in the wilderness? There is no bread! There is no water! And we detest this miserable food!"
>
> Then the LORD sent venomous snakes among them; they bit the people, and many Israelites died. The people came to Moses and said, "We sinned when we spoke against the LORD and against you. Pray that the LORD will take the snakes away from us." So, Moses prayed for the people.
>
> The LORD said to Moses, "Make a snake and put it up on a pole; anyone who is bitten can look at it and live." So, Moses made a bronze snake and put it up on a pole. Then, when anyone was bitten by a snake and looked at the bronze snake, they lived.

The Israelites were not satisfied with God or Moses at this point, and began to complain, not trusting in God's process for their journey. Their faith began to weaken. Their dissatisfaction with God's provision of manna reflects a deeper issue of trust and gratitude. The venomous snakes symbolize the consequences of sin and rebellion against God.

The story, in itself, demonstrates that God offers both judgment and mercy to all who "look up" to Him. Hebrews 12:2a reminds us to fix our eyes on Jesus, the pioneer and perfecter of faith. God wants us to focus our attention on Him, rather than dwelling on our current circumstances, trusting that God is in control even when things seem difficult. Picture the situation: venomous snakes everywhere, nowhere to turn, bitten, your situation is severe, you're suffering terribly, and perhaps dying. Now, in this scenario, where would you look? Well, a natural reaction would be to look down and watch your footing to avoid stepping on a serpent, or better yet, avoid being bitten.

God instructed Moses to create a bronze serpent and wrap it around the pole. This concept is the source for the ancient figure of healing and medicine, which has influenced the adoption of the serpent and pole, which is known as the "Rod of Asclepius." The American Medical Association (AMA) has used the Rod of Asclepius as its logo since 2005, and it is widely used by other medical organizations and institutions throughout the Western World.

The bronze snake serves as a powerful symbol of salvation and healing. Those who looked at the bronze snake were saved from death, foreshadowing themes of healing and redemption. This act of looking at the bronze snake can be seen as an act of faith, believing that God's provision would bring healing.

The connection between the serpent on the pole in Numbers 21 and the symbol of medicine lies in the themes of healing and salvation. In the biblical account, looking at the bronze serpent was an indication for the Israelites to be healed from the deadly bites of the snakes, serving as a metaphor for faith and divine healing. God has a funny way of making us laugh. The cure was simple: "look up" to the serpent to be healed, the very thing that created your situation. God wants us to look up and get our eyes off our circumstances: sickness, distress, finances, etc. There wasn't any healing in the serpent on the pole; the healing came from obeying the command, "look up." Looking up to God Almighty for all our needs, He's a healer, deliverer, provider, and sustainer.

If God had willed it, healing would have been instantaneously by "the Word." However, God didn't command them to touch the serpent, pray, or call the elders of the church; all He wanted them to do was "look up" and live.

In Christian theology, this passage is often interpreted as foreshadowing the crucifixion of Jesus Christ. Just as the Israelites looked at the bronze serpent to be healed, believers are called to look to Christ for spiritual healing and salvation. Jesus himself referenced this event in John 3:14-15, where He said, "Just as Moses lifted up the snake in the wilderness, so the Son of Man must be lifted up, that everyone who believes may have eternal life in him."

> *Dear God, help us to be obedient to Your Word and to Your will, to listen when You speak, and have the strength to follow Your plans for our lives, even when we can't see the end result. May we trust You and keep looking to You for bountiful mercies in Your son Jesus' name. We count it done, Amen.*

I am the Art Instructor at Kingstree High School with a passion for nurturing creativity and inspiring young artists. Coming from a family with a strong artistic heritage, I bring a rich history of creativity to my role. Prior to my career in education, I dedicated 25 years to nursing as a Licensed Practical Nurse (LPN) until my journey was redirected by a diagnosis of Multiple Myeloma and two Bone Marrow Transplants. As a mother of four adult children and a proud grandmother of sixteen grandchildren, family and serving God remain at the heart of my life's journey.

As a Certified Lay Servant of the United Methodist Conference and a current member of St. Michael's Reformed Episcopal church, I serve in the capacity of Missionary chairperson, choir member, vestry board member, and avid Bible scholar. I find joy in sharing my faith and knowledge with others. In my free time, I indulge in my love of traveling, drawing, photography, exploring new cultures, and creating lasting memories among my friends and with my family. – Vernesa Penny Green

Let Go and Let God

Carol Raftis

> Be anxious for nothing, but in everything by prayer and supplication, with thanksgiving, let your requests be made known to God. Philippians 4:6

    I was a special needs teacher for thirty years, and I accumulated and held onto so much stuff that I needed a storage unit. The unit was medium-sized and was packed with boxes full of material that I used to teach my students. I was working on the unit for years with no real results in clearing it. I held on so long that I had forgotten what some of the material was, but I needed to hold onto it. After retirement, spending the extra money on a storage unit became a financial burden on me. It became very stressful, and I was so anxious until it became paralyzing, and I felt like a noose was around my neck. I would often cry. It was a hidden secret, and for a long time, I was not willing to ask for help.

    Because of God's faithfulness, tender mercies, and answered prayer, I was invited to join an intercessory prayer line with a group of faithful men and women who prayed for me again and again. I sought the Lord because I needed spiritual and physical help, and the Lord provided both. God gave me the strategy and my helper, and I packed the material in the car, brought it to my house, and put it in the garage, which actually added to the anxiety and stress because I could not put my car in the garage. But we kept at it, and we put the boxes on plastic shelves and organized them. Even though we cleaned the storage unit and organized the material, I was still not ready to let it go. I wanted it to go to a place where it would be used and appreciated, I wanted it to go to a good home. The stress and anxiety of holding onto it was real, and as I continually joined these intercessors seeking help and receiving encouragement, the Lord gave me a word of wisdom, "Let it go, it has served its purpose." That word gave me the courage and strength to let it go. We found places to donate the material where it would be used, and I was able to put my car back in the garage.

God took me through a "process" of deliverance from anxiousness and stress. He opened my eyes to the things I was letting keep me in bondage. I was not willing to ask for help, which can be a sign of pride. The teaching material had become a part of my identity because I loved teaching so much. I realized that holding onto the materials was an addiction and fear. My seeking God for help and the prayers I received helped me to break strongholds from a dysfunctional childhood. I've learned and would like to share that whatever is causing you to be anxious, stressed, and fearful, God has the solution in his word.

> Be anxious for nothing, but in everything by prayer and supplication, with thanksgiving, let your requests be made known to God. Philippians 4:6
>
> I sought the Lord; He heard me and delivered me from all my fears. Psalm 34:4

Carol Raftis has a master's degree in ESL and Special Education with 32 years of teaching disadvantaged urban youth. She is a mother of three children with six grandchildren. She has been born-again for 12 years and is a member of Global Compass Prayer Ministries and Deliverance Intercessors Prayer Ministry, with a special focus on praying for youth.

A Woman and a Well

Rev. Easter Frazier

> Everyone who drinks of this water will thirst again; but whoever drinks of the water that I will give him shall never thirst; but the water that I will give him will become in him a well of water springing up to eternal life. John 4:13-14, NIV

Prophetic Word from Graham Cook given to me in 1996:

"Easter, there is a strong leadership gift on your life. God is saying: don't go back from that because of bad experiences. Go and run with it. Go, get in the race again, because God trusts you. He will give you wisdom.

There is a very strong prophetic Spirit on your life; a capacity to intercede and pray into being the things that are not. That is an important part of your life and ministry. There are signs and wonders around your life. A supernatural anointing upon your life and ministry; God has gifted you to preach. You should preach and teach. God is going to open your heart and give you tremendous REVELATION.

I see you traveling in company with other people, to different countries.

There is a strong releasing anointing upon your life, to equip and train and to release, and particularly to release people from bondages and hurts and wounds and cause them to move on from where they are from the things that bothered them. In fact, there is a SWORD that works in your life that cuts chains off

> people, there is another part of your life that gives them meaning and purpose to get involved in things. And so, you are always going to be in demand, particularly at conferences and seminars and things like that.
>
> There is a powerful IMPARTATION in your hands, POWERFUL IMPARTATION. You should lay hands on people. But from this point on, God is saying, when you lay hands on people, understand the ANOINTING that I am giving you: When you lay hands on people, you will get insight, you will get wisdom." End of prophetic word!!!

Called to the Nations: Cameroon

I was called into Africa through a prophetic word. In November 2000, Pastor David T. Demola of Faith Fellowship Ministries World Outreach Center (FFMWOC) called me forward and gave me a prophetic word that I would go to Africa and minister. Pastor Billy Lubansa was present at FFMWOC, visiting from Africa. Pastor Dave called him up and proclaimed to him that he needed to have me, this woman of God, to come to his country (Cameroon) and minister to the women there. Pastor Dave said: This is a powerful woman of God.

In March 2001, I was invited as a speaker to Pastor Lubansa's large Fire Conference in Cameroon, Africa. Funds were needed to fulfill this prophetic word.

The FISH!

Before I went to Cameroon, I had a prayer meeting in my home, and my friend came to the prayer meeting. We talked about my going to Cameroon and the need to raise funds. In addition, my taxes were due at that time. We prayed and heard "fish." We decided to step out in faith and go fishing. (Matthew 17:27, NIV) "But so that we may not cause offense, go to the lake, and throw out your line. Take the first fish you catch; open its mouth and you will find a four-drachma coin. Take it and give it to them for my tax and yours."

The next day, we went to a fish market to buy fish. We purchased the fish. Imagine our chagrin when we brought the fish home and realized that it had already been gutted and cleaned.

We went to the service that evening at FFMWOC, and Pastor Dave called me up. He asked the people to donate to the trip to Cameroon and to the need that I had in my life at that time, which was to pay my taxes. That's why we bought the fish earlier in the day. We believed by faith that the FISH would have a coin in its mouth. God honored our faith to believe in Him and obey. After Pastor Dave called me up, the people sowed enough for the trip and to pay my taxes. My God honored our faith!!!

I had not been to Africa before. The Lord chose a dear friend to travel with me, Rev. Hazel Hector. Excitement and some fear, and anxiety flooded my heart. I quote Robert T. Bennett as he exhorted, "Don't be pushed around by the fears in your mind. Be led by the dreams in your heart."

WHEN I CAN'T, GOD CAN!!!!

During this season, I was being tremendously blessed by a ministry called Eagles Wings led by Robert Stearns. Their worship released, whether live or recorded, was deep and passionate. I knew it would be an awesome opening of the atmosphere before I ministered God's word. I was so nervous seeing the number of people, but confident that I had heard God. The song released was Undiscovered Country.

One of my most memorable experiences was the response of the people to the sound of that song in the air. When I play this song now, I'm brought right back to Cameroon and seeing the faces of the people. The sound and the anointing filled the atmosphere. People stood and raised their hands in honor of the King of Glory. His presence and anointing were tangible. I declared to them that I was a sign to them; a miracle representing what God can do in their lives. I'm not sure how many had seen an American woman preacher who looked like them.

I declared, even now, that I was a sign. Many pieces had come together for me to stand and preach in Cameroon. Yes, my presence was a sign from God! It is a miracle!!!

> Therefore, with joy, you will draw water from the wells of salvation. Isaiah 12:3 NKJV

Uganda

Fast forward to 2014, when I met Pastor Paul Musisi from Uganda. He shared his testimony and life's work with me. I had been to Uganda in 2011 and observed the conditions and widespread lack of safe, clean drinking water. I learned from Pastor Musisi that he had to purchase water. I likened it to how I purchase oil for my home furnace. It was very expensive!

I knew that God was moving my heart to get involved somehow. The more we talked, the more I understood the serious need and what I was to do.

One of the facts that moved me was that girls are the major ones responsible for getting water for a household. It can take up to 6 hours per day to get enough water. This leaves no time for these girls to go to school. That is a big problem. Having grown up in Alabama, the daughter of a sharecropper, I know how important an education is to break the cycle of poverty and lack.

God created me to make a difference. Drilling a well that would serve a community would make a tremendous difference. Therefore, I said YES to Pastor Musisi.

Robert T. Bennett provided further inspiration as he said, "Success is not how high you have climbed, but how you make a positive difference to the world." The world of Pastor Musisi, his staff, and over 250 children in only one of his locations would be changed forever with a clean, safe drinking water well.

I had no clue how to drill the drinking water well. I researched organizations that were involved in the process of drilling wells. After a while, I realized that God wanted me to get this well drilled and have full responsibility for the assignment from beginning to end.

I have a team that I've prayed with for over 25 years. We began to pray and intercede around the assignment of DRILLING a safe, clean drinking water well in Uganda. God was doing something special. As Jesus said, "And whoever in the name of a disciple gives to one of these little ones even a cup of cold water to drink, truly I say to you, he shall not lose his reward." (Matthew 10:42, NIV)

God's tapestry of divine connections over a lifetime was now giving life to a people in need. I knew a few people in Uganda from my last mission trip. I called one of them; Isaac Mukisa, who referred me to a Driller in Kampala Uganda.

God's divine wisdom guided the process of protecting our interests and secured Kasthew Group Co. Ltd. of Kampala, Uganda, as the company to drill the well. In addition, a dear friend and colleague connected me with Jerry F. Vorbach, P.E., MBA (an engineer in New Jersey), who was secured as the project manager representing In Him Ministries, Inc.

Many fundraising events were held, and people caught the vision and sowed very generously into the expense of drilling the drinking water well in Uganda.

We were able to give life-giving water to the people of Uganda, in every sense of the word! As Jesus put it, "Everyone who drinks of this water will thirst again; but whoever drinks of the water that I will give him shall never thirst; but the water that I will give him will become in him a well of water springing up to eternal life."

(John 4:13-14, NIV) What a privilege to minister to both the people's physical as well as spiritual needs.

In early April 2017, Engineer Jerry flew to Uganda and began the project. The well was finished on Good Friday of 2017. In July, we traveled to Uganda to dedicate the finished drinking water well!!! What an awesome Journey!!!

The joy of knowing that God trusted me to get a safe, clean drinking water well for the children and people in that section of Uganda can't be fully expressed. Great Joy!

Rev. Easter G. Frazier was awarded the New Jersey State Governor's Jefferson Award for Public Service on June 2, 2018, for her work in securing safe, clean drinking water for the children of Uganda.

Manifest! Manifest! Manifest!

Dr. Merilyn V. Davis

Many of us are familiar with a song sung in some of our church services. It speaks of prayers prayed long ago. Perhaps an ancestor, grandparent, parent, pastor, or even a teacher thought about you, lifted you before the Father, and interceded for you.

Somebody Prayed for Me...

Maybe they sent up the timber for your prosperity or your healing. They petitioned for your mental, physical, or even emotional well-being.

They prayed that God's favor shines upon you, that Jehovah Shalom gives you His peace that surpasses all understanding, and that your financial security is in the hands of Jehovah Jireh, the Divine Provider.

They prayed that your life and your footsteps would be orchestrated from the Throne Room in heaven!

Even right now today, those very prayers that were sometimes prayed to the point of travail are carrying you through, feeding you, sheltering you, healing you, protecting you, keeping you, and building up your most radical faith.

You are living in time, beyond time, of those very prayers.

Centuries-old prayers.

Generations-gone-by prayers. Prayers of yesteryear, and yesterday. Prayers for you, through the pain, tears, and fears of ancient prayer warriors. Prayers borne of they knew not what but birthed in earnest and of one's personal experiences.

Prayers for you, of whom not only did they not know, but of whom they would never know, outside of the confines of Spirit. Prayers uttered from way down deep within their very souls, through the supernatural.

Sometimes, the prayers could not even be verbally articulated. They emerged from the depths of their belly in incoherent moans, groans, hymns, and hums.

Romans 8:26 reveals the prayers of divine intercession. In the King James Version of the Bible, Romans 8:26 says, "But the Spirit itself maketh intercession for us with groanings which cannot be uttered."

Reverend Dr. Merilyn V. Davis, Kingdom Woman

Pastor, Prophet, Gospel Preacher, Bestselling Author, Speaker, Podcaster, Radio Executive Producer, and Talk-show Host. Everywhere her voice is heard, somebody's eyes are opened, and somebody's life is changed. Dr. Davis brings you to the juxtaposition of Kingdom and Culture.

Dr. Davis was awarded the Honorary Doctorate Degree of Humanitarianism in 2023 and the Presidential Lifetime Achievement Award in 2024.

To request her for your next virtual or in-person event, in ministry, or the marketplace, and for additional information, connect with her on her app: BookMerilynDavis.com.

Abandoned but not Forgotten

Diana Stevens

> Though my father and my mother forsake me, the Lord will receive me. Teach me your way, O Lord; lead me in a straight path because of my oppressors. Psalm 27:10 NIV

Back in 1967, I went off to school, and I was called to the office to go home. I had no idea what was going on or what was awaiting me. When I arrived home, I saw all these strange people in the house with cameras, and they began to take photos of us. At the time, I couldn't comprehend what was going on, but later in life, I found out what happened. I was removed from my biological parents and placed with a foster family. I was seven years old at the time and didn't have a clue about what was going on. All I remembered at that time was the pictures being taken of us, which depicted a false story. The name of the Agency was the Division of Youth and Family Services (DYFS). I was hospitalized and diagnosed with walking pneumonia. Still afraid and not knowing what was happening, I felt so alone, rejected, and abandoned. But God! God ensured that I was placed in a loving home, and as a child, I learned a lot and grew stronger. I accepted Jesus at the age of 8 years old, and today I am still serving Him at age 64. In John 1:12-13 NIV, it states, "Yet to all who received Him, to those who believed in His name, He gave the right to become children of God, children born not of natural descent, nor of human decision or a husband's will, but born of God." I am so glad God decided in advance to adopt us into His own family by bringing us to Himself through Jesus Christ (Ephesians 1:5).

So, for all of you out there, who were ever told you are nothing, or you will never be anything; if you're feeling friendless, feeling lonely or even worried about how your life will turn out; let's all take God at His Word when He says, " The Lord Himself goes before you and will be with you; He will never leave you nor forsake you. Do not be afraid; do not be discouraged. (Deuteronomy 31:8).

Even before God made the world, God loved us and chose us in Christ to be holy and without fault in His eyes. God decided in advance to adopt us into His own family by bringing us to Himself through Christ Jesus. This is what He wanted to do, and it gave Him great pleasure.

So, we praise God for the glorious grace He has poured out on us who belong to His dear Son. (Ephesians 1:4-6)

Most gracious Father, thank You for adoption, which is a beautiful example of Your love for us. Just as adoptive parents make a choice to give a child a new life, so You choose to give us a new life in You that we could not achieve on our own. Those who choose to adopt children choose to lovingly teach and nurture them and give them the rights and privileges that come with being a member of their family. Father God, You have done the same for us and we are forever grateful. God, we praise You, and give You the honor, glory, and the highest praise! We are so privileged to receive all of Your Love and blessings.

Heavenly Father, thank You for choosing us to be part of Your family. Remind us that no matter what challenges we face, You are with us, encouraging, guiding, protecting, and cheering us on. Thank You for showing Your unconditional love to us through adoption. Thank You God for loving us so well!

In Jesus' Name, Amen.

Diana Stevens grew up surrounded by a Christian family. She accepted Jesus Christ as her Lord and Savior when she was 8 years old and was active in church activities through her entire youth.

In college, her faith continued to mature, and she was involved in on-campus Christian Fellowship Meetings. She is an Elder and Usher at the Love of Jesus Family Church. She loves being a servant of God and serving His people. Her favorite garment to put on is "Love."

In her free time, she enjoys ministering to God's people and likes crochet, sewing, and studying the Word of God. She fellowships at the Love of Jesus Family Church and is a prayer leader with Global Compass Prayer Ministries.

You can contact Diana at givekindness777@gmail.com

Trust the Lord

Darcel Lowery

> Trust in the Lord with all thine heart and lean not to thy own understanding. In all your ways acknowledge Him, and He shall direct thy paths. Proverbs 3: 5 – 6

In the Bible, trust is defined as a confident belief in the truth, reliability, ability, or strength of something or someone.

The Bible mentions the word trust 193 times, and the words translated as trust come from at least twenty different original language words. The Greek word for trust, "pistis," appears 243 times in the New Testament alone. This tells you how important it is to put your trust in the Lord.

There are times when you just have to trust the Lord to lead and direct you. When you do, He will let you know it was only He who brought you through. That trust starts with a commitment to Him and knowing He will never lead you down the wrong path. If He is directing your life, He is faithful to fulfill and provide you with the tools, support, strength, knowledge, and wisdom to do what He desires you to do. God's word is trustworthy. His plans for you are perfect and purposeful. Why wouldn't you trust Him?

I remember a time in my life when I stepped out on faith and trusted the Lord. He told me to do something that I just knew I couldn't do, and for that matter, others told me I couldn't do it, as well.

I went to high school during a time when guidance counselors advised you on a career path based on aptitude tests. Coming out of high school, I wanted to go to college, but my high school counselor advised me against it. I was told I wouldn't be successful and would be better suited for a secretarial career (I really wasn't a good typist).

Needless to say, I followed the path my counselor suggested until one day, layoffs were considered at my job. God told me to go to college. This was something I did not want to do because of my high school experience. I dropped out of college prep courses, I did not pass Algebra, and my guidance counselor said I wasn't college material.

One Sunday, a guest Minister prophesied, "... someone needs to go back to school ..." I knew that it was the Lord talking directly to me! The next day, I registered to begin my college career, trusting God but never expecting how he was going to BLESS ME!

With the help of others, I passed the college prep courses I dropped and couldn't pass in high school. God poured wisdom into me as I "studied to show myself approved." Accolades from professors gave me confidence, but I knew that my accomplishments were only made possible with the Lord's help.

Long story short, (God blessed me in so many ways during my college career, too many to recount here), not only did I achieve a college degree but a graduate degree as well with an academic honor of Summa Cum Laude. I also accepted a teaching position at my college just days before my graduation. I have been teaching at my alma mater for over 20 years now, all because I trusted God! When others said I couldn't ... God said ... You Will!

Is there something you need to trust the Lord for? Why not stand on your faith? God is faithful to do what He said He would do. He will never leave you nor forsake you. If God puts something in your heart to do, He will send the resources and support you need to accomplish it. Step out on faith and "Trust in the Lord!"

> The Lord is my strength and my shield; my heart trusteth in Him, and I am helped; therefore, my heart greatly rejoiceth; and with my song I will praise Him.
> Psalm 28:7

Darcel Lowery, MHRM, is a prayer leader with Global Compass Prayer Ministry with a master's degree in human resource management. She is an Account Manager for A to Z Insurance Agency and is a part-time lecturer for Rutgers University, New Brunswick, New Jersey.

The Life of an Intercessory Prayer Warrior

Global Compass
Prayer Ministries Inc.

Trusting God in A Challenging Time

Rev. Dr. Claire P. Higgins

Define Trust: Merriam-Webster says, "It is a firm belief in the reliability, truth, ability, or strength of someone or something."

Strong's definition says: "To trust; to hope; to make someone a refuge."

We who are believers are aware that trust is built through fellowship, honesty, and sincerity. Because we have the love of Jesus Christ in our hearts, there's nothing we would deliberately do to hurt others. Do you have an experience to reflect on where you lost trust in someone?

During our lives, we have experienced times when our trust has been broken. As believers, we may have been disappointed because the bond of fellowship, where someone showed compassion and sincerity toward us, was crushed.

No experience is hidden from God. He is aware of every moment and watches over every situation we go through in this life. We need to put our complete trust in Him, for He is the only one who knows what's best for us.

> For I know the plans I have for you," declares the Lord, "plans to prosper you and not harm you, plans to give you hope and a future. Jeremiah 29:11

On this journey called life, the greatest struggle is to trust God. It's easy to trust God when the sun is shining on your side of the street. You know the outcome, and you feel at peace because everything is going just like clockwork. All is well at home, at your job, and your finances are in order. There is no problem trusting the Lord. Your mountain has been removed, and you're singing the song of victory. But are you able to trust God when you are in a valley of despair?

How can you trust God when you don't know where the money is coming from to pay the next bill or food for the next meal, or when your marriage is collapsing? How do you trust God when your children have backslidden? How do you trust God when you've been given a medical diagnosis that causes you to leave your career?

When these things happen, it's difficult to trust God. Great despair can be overwhelming. But God hasn't asked us to do something impossible. The Lord has given us many scriptures that we can walk in and rely on. I believe that as we draw near to Him, we will become confident in trusting Him with every area of our lives.

There Are Patriarchs in the Bible Who Show Us How They Trusted God in Challenging Times:

1. Joseph – Genesis 37:1–47:37
   Joseph trusted God and understood his calling through dreams.
2. Moses – Exodus 1:21, 3:2–10
   Moses trusted the Lord when he saw the burning bush.

3. Ruth - Ruth 1:8–22
   Ruth trusted the Lord and left her kindred to follow Naomi.
4. Job – Job 1:1–42:16, 13:15
   Job trusted the Lord even after losing all he owned.
5. Jesus – Matthew 6:25, Luke 22:42, Mark 5:36
   Jesus is the prime example of trusting God.
6. The Woman with the Issue of Blood – Luke 8:48
   This woman showed strong trust in receiving her divine healing.
7. Apostle Paul – 2 Corinthians 12:9
   Paul trusted God's grace even though the thorn was not removed.

Eight Keys to Help Us Trust the Lord

1. Don't Trust Yourself
   - Proverbs 3:5 TPT
     Trust in the Lord completely and do not rely on your own opinions. With all your heart, rely on Him to guide you, and He will lead you in every decision you make.
2. Keep Your Confession Updated
   - Repent – Psalm 51:10 NKJV
     Create in me a clean heart, O God, and renew a steadfast spirit within me.
   - Forgiveness
     Tolerate the weakness of those in the family of faith, forgiving one another in the same way Jesus Christ has graciously forgiven you.

3. Seek the Lord
   - Psalm 119:105 NKJV
     Your word is a lamp to my feet and a light to my path.
4. Flee from All Evil
   - 1 John 2:16 TPT
     For all that the world can offer us—the gratification of our flesh, the allurement of things of the world, and the obsession with status and importance—none of these things come from the Father but from the world.
   - Proverbs 3:7 TPT
     Don't think for a moment that you know it all, for wisdom comes when you adore Him with undivided devotion and avoid everything that's wrong.
5. Let God Be the Head of Your Life
   - Matthew 6:33 NKJV
     But seek first the kingdom of God and His righteousness, and all these things shall be added to you.
6. Use God's Word as Your Compass
7. Tune Your Ears with the Holy Spirit
   - Romans 8:6 NKJV
     For to be carnally minded is death, but to be spiritually minded is life and peace.
8. Let God's Love Bring You Rest and Comfort
   - Isaiah 41:10 NKJV
     Fear not, for I am with you; be not dismayed, for I am your God. I will strengthen you, yes, I will help you, I will uphold you with My righteous right hand.

As our relationship becomes stronger, we will be able to trust Him with our loved ones and bring to Him every issue in our lives. We will have the assurance that whatever is going on, the Lord knows, and He cares. The perfect love He has for us will bring peace, glory, and honor to His name.

> Every evening, I will explain my need to Him. Every morning, I will move my soul toward Him. Every waking hour I will worship only Him, and He will hear and respond to my cry. Psalm 55:17 TPT

May the Bible study strengthen your relationship with the Lord. May you trust our Jehovah and allow His leading to bring you to a place of trusting Him in every challenging situation.

Rev. Dr. Claire P. Higgins is a native of Philadelphia, PA, born to William and Clarine Lewis. She accepted Jesus Christ as her Savior at the age of twelve. He gifted her to sing the Gospel at an early age. Claire heard the call of God in March 2003, under the pastorate of Reverend Lynda T. Rassmann at Grants A.M.E. Church.

Claire was ordained under the leadership of Doctor Willie Mae Robinson in May 2004 and also received an ordination with the International Ministerial Fellowship in June 2004. As she pursued her studies, she received her Master's in Theology and Doctor of Divinity in June 2014. In November 2020, Claire founded the Deliverance Intercessor Prayer Ministry.

Claire is also a retired nurse and the proud mother of three sons, two daughters-in-love, and three grandchildren.

Small Group Praying

Pastor Freddie Williams

There are times in your life when the thing that you don't want to happen is the very thing that happens. There are times when something you desire seems like an impossibility. You don't want to learn that you are losing your job; however, if you are informed of this possibility, what is the course of action? You don't want to hear that you must wait for the promotion; however, if you are informed of this possibility, then what is the course of action? Might I recommend prayer? In my times of indirection, I've found that when I have made time to pray, I have gained the direction that I was seeking.

Prayer isn't a last resort or last-ditch effort in response to a seemingly hopeless situation. No, in fact, prayer is a posture of confidence in the One to whom you are submitting your prayers. That's the secret power of prayer. Prayer, when used to communicate with our God, is the most effective tool that we have to navigate this thing called life.

I remember in 2003 when I moved to North Carolina, fresh from graduating from college, my cousin hosted a small group Bible study at her house. They met in her living room, fellowshipping and growing in their faith. At the end of their meeting, the facilitator would ask if there were prayer requests, and a designated person in the group would write them down. After everyone shared their requests and they were recorded in the hearing of all, each person would hold hands, and the small group leader began to pray. The facilitator prayed over the recorded requests of each person in the group and even over the requests left unspoken. Even though the person might not have shared that heartfelt, unspoken wish with the group, it wasn't hidden from the Lord. Just being in the group, holding the hand of the person beside them, was enough for connection with God through His Spirit.

The following year, instead of going upstairs and avoiding the people, I joined that small group at my cousin's home. I'm pretty sure my cousin prayed that everything in her house would be used for the glory of God. When I joined the prayer group, I noticed how tightly knit everyone was and how welcoming they were to me. We opened the small group meetings with a shared meal, followed by worship and a lesson for the evening. At the end of the meetings, we were asked if we had any prayer requests. This is where I gained the most direction I have ever encountered in my life. This is what kept me coming back to small group Bible study.

One thing really stood out to me that I'd like to share.

> These all with one mind were continually devoting themselves to prayer. Acts 1:14

As the first church met in small groups in homes, they devoted themselves to prayer. As Jesus left his disciples with His Spirit and the command and commission to go and make disciples, they went. As they went, the Holy Spirit directed the disciples and empowered them to share the good news of Jesus. This being the first century, the people remembered Jesus of Nazareth and his miracles. As the disciples were leading, they were praying, and people were added to their numbers daily. They were seeing answered prayers, and the disciples started a community where they met the needs of each person in the group. One of the main characteristics of this group was prayer. The Bible tells us they came together with one mind, devoting themselves to prayer. They got together and prayed to the Lord God. He provided direction. He kept them and granted them power to perform His will. Inside this community, people found family, acceptance, and the answers to their prayers.

Prayer in a small group of like-minded believers is a powerful tool that can help you get to where God wants you to be. When we allow God's Spirit to meet us in a group setting, the power quotient multiplies. God moves in people's lives in a way that just doesn't happen when we're alone. God answers our prayers in our prayer time alone with Him, and He provides even more benefits when an assembly of His children pray together with like-mindedness and persistence.

> These all with one mind were continually devoting themselves to prayer.
>
> New American Standard Bible: 1995 Update (La Habra, CA: The Lockman Foundation, 1995) Acts 1:14

Freddie Williams is a pastor from Charlotte, North Carolina, by way of Beckley, West Virginia, with a bachelor's degree in chemistry from West Virginia State University. Freddie is married to Brandi Williams, and together, they have four children. He serves as the Lead Pastor for LightWay Church, a church located in the Steele Creek area of Charlotte, NC. You can contact him at pastor.freddie@lightway.church or visit the church website at www.LightWay.church

Living in Peace on Purpose

Linda B. Johnson

The dictionary defines peace as freedom from disturbance or tranquility. Another definition is a state or period in which there is no war, or a war has ended. The definition of "on purpose" is to do something intentionally, deliberately, consciously, and willingly.

God and the world's meaning of peace are so different. The world believes that peace is the absence of trouble, problems, conflict, controversy, sickness, and heartbreak. However, the peace of God goes beyond worldly peace, because Our Father's peace is within us, through the Holy Spirit, even when those things are present. God is either going to take us out of the situation or take us through it. As we are going through it, if we trust Him and draw nigh to Him, He will give us a calm that the world knows nothing about. The difference between the world's peace and God's peace is that God's peace is not contingent on the situation or circumstances; it is contingent on our trust in God.

> I have told you these things, so that in me you may have peace. In this world, you will have trouble. But take heart! I have overcome the world. John 16:33

We must tell ourselves that we will be intentional about living and being in peace. Let's get up deliberately seeking peace for that day. Let us lay down at night consciously seeking peace for a good night's sleep.

We sometimes take peace for granted until we turn around one day and find it's gone.

Let's talk about the world system for a minute. The news media, social media, music industry, psychics, and government continue to cause fear, anxiety, panic, and depression. The enemy wants to strip us of our peace by infiltrating our minds. We must protect our ear and eye gates and be careful of what we let come in. The Word of God tells us:

> Casting down imaginations, and every high thing that exalteth itself against the knowledge of God and bringing into captivity every thought to the obedience of Christ. 2 Corinthians 10:5

Our mental health is just as important, if not more, as our physical health. People exercise at home, walk, go to the gym, run marathons, and so many other things to stay fit or to lose weight. But what do we do to stay spiritually fit? How often do we study and meditate on the Word of God, pray, and fast to get closer to God?

First, we need to lose weight spiritually. We will never be able to have peace carrying around the weight of sin, guilt, and shame. So, let us let it go, give it to God, and He will give us peace.

> Lay aside every weight and the sin which doth so easily beset us. Hebrew 12:1

In Isaiah, it tells us that we can have perfect (completed, real, total, absolute, without fault) peace. How can we do this? We can do it by keeping our minds held fast on God and the things of God. We can do it by trusting in Him, totally!

> Thou wilt keep him in perfect peace,
> whose mind is stayed on thee:
> because he trusteth in thee. Isaiah 26:3

In God, we find a peace that no man can give us or take away from us. It's a peace that is unexplainable, supernatural, and can't be penetrated. This peace won't only keep our minds, but it will keep and protect our hearts. It exceeds any and everything the world could ever give us.

> And the peace of God, which passeth all understanding, shall keep your hearts and minds through Christ Jesus. Philippians 4:7

This peace enables us to lie down at night in peace and get up in the morning in peace. We have the assurance that we are safe in the arms of the Master. Being secure and safe is important to us all. We can only find it in God.

> I will both lay me down in peace, and sleep:
> for thou, Lord, only makest me dwell in safety.
> Psalm 4:8

Lord, help us all learn to value the peace of God. Something that we value, we will do whatever it takes to keep it. Let this be our prayer for one another.

> The Lord bless thee and keep thee:
> The Lord make His face shine upon thee, and be gracious unto thee:
> The Lord lift up His countenance upon thee and give thee peace. Numbers 6:24-26

> *When peace like a river attendeth my way*
>
> *When sorrows like sea billows roll*
>
> *Whatever my lot, Thou has taught me to say*
>
> *It is well, it is well with my soul.*
>
> *Horatio G. Spafford, 1828-1888*

I have a personal testimony regarding peace.

My three siblings and I were born to our loving parents in Youngstown, Ohio. We did everything together – traveled, sang, and ministered. I accepted Jesus as my Lord and Savior at an early age, and He filled my heart with so much love for other people. However, I was very naïve and didn't realize that I wouldn't always receive love back.

At the age of twenty-four, I married and moved to Rochester, New York. It was very hard because I didn't have family there and I missed them so much.

When my firstborn was 6 months old, the domestic violence started, and because I didn't really know who I was in the Lord, I stayed in it for 17 years. I was like a ship without a sail, being tossed back and forth. There were many points in my life where I felt like I was losing my mind – BUT GOD!!!

I thank God for how, when I totally surrendered to Him, He came in and showed me that He was my peace in the midst of a storm. He taught me how to ride the waves and assured me I was safe in His arms. All I know is that I am a living, walking miracle. Having peace is worth more than any worldly possessions will ever be.

In conclusion, I would like to challenge you to take time out daily to commune with God on a much deeper level. Study His Word so that "He can be a lamp unto your feet and a light unto your path" (Psalm 119:105).

> And Peter answered Him and said, Lord, if it be thou, bid me come unto thee on the water.
>
> And He said, Come. And when Peter was come down out of the ship, He walked on the water to go to Jesus.
>
> But when He saw the wind boisterous, He was afraid; and beginning to sink, He cried, saying, Lord, save me.
>
> And immediately Jesus stretched forth His hand, and caught Him, and said unto him, O thou of little faith, wherefore didst thou doubt? Matthew 14:28-31

Peter was fine until he took his focus off Jesus and put it on the storm. When Peter said, "Save me," he was already close enough for Jesus to stretch out His hand and catch him. I want to encourage you not to give up because your breakthrough is just that close. Jesus wants to be your peace in the midst of your storm.

There may be storms all around you but make a decree not to let them inside you. Remember, true peace comes when you choose to live for Jesus Christ.

TODAY I LIVE IN PEACE ON PURPOSE!

> Peace I leave with you, my peace I give unto you: not as the world giveth, give I unto you. Let not your heart be troubled, neither let it be afraid. John 14:27
>
> For to be carnally minded is death; but to be spiritually minded is life and peace. Romans 8:6
>
> When thou liest down, thou shalt not be afraid: yea, thou shalt lie down, and thy sleep shall be sweet. Proverbs 3:24

My name is Linda B. Johnson. I was born in Youngstown, Ohio, and currently reside in Rochester, New York. I have an associate's degree in business administration. I am a member, praise team leader, an elder, and Sunday School Superintendent at New Born Fellowship Church, Inc. My pastors are Drs. Warren and Perdita Meeks.

Email: lindabirdgriffin@gmail.com
Facebook: Linda Bernice Griffin
Instagram: lindabgriffin60

The Perfect Quilt of Prayer With Jesus

Rev. Ellen Carter Haygood

In this episode of praise, hope, and love, proactive committed partners of our intercessory prayer group became engaged one by one for those in need of the many things we pray for each week. We are woven together as a beautiful quilt of love, warmth, and security filled with the inner[1] confident hope of being heard by a loving Lord through the Holy Spirit. Pieced together one by one, arriving in the group at different times, each of us enters with the anticipation of being used while also seeking grace. We are joined together with the common thread of[2] believers in a Christ who uses anyone willing to come;[2] yet the fibers of each vary in texture and are of different colors. It is a great reminder from the story of Joseph's colorful coat that can symbolize the divine favor of each person with the promise of a better life.[3] The coat of many colors is a reminder of the promise of divine grace and favor, and God's love for each and every person in the quilt prayer group, allowing each person to understand and know we are involved in doing the work. No matter how big or how small, it matters to God in a huge way. We need each other. The call to pray is for the cry of the hurt, the suffering, and those in agony seeking healing, peace, and comfort.

The Open Door Quilt Gathering

The quilt prayer group started with Sarah and Maya when they began praying for their sick grandmother Amelia. Soon, there were eight committed to coming out and praying weekly at the same time. They prayed for needs as they occurred. Sickness, work, children, a home, a grant for school, safe travels, family in the military, safe pregnancy, mending a relationship, healing from cancer, success in a procedure or operation, for adult children with epilepsy, for those struggling with infidelity in marriage. Annette, who came for the first time, requested prayer for her neighbor's son, who ran away from home over a week ago and has not been located.

The group is now up to thirty-five members of all ages attending almost all meetings as we embrace the magnificence of how God is using us and see the manifestation of Jesus in how prayers have been answered. Each person either comes with a cloth or receives one when they enter. Every time we pray for a particular need, we choose a color thread and sew our cloth into part of the quilt. Now the quilt is thirty-six inches in width and forty-six inches in length.

We celebrate with thanksgiving when someone shares a victory with a bright red cloth, which we sew into the last piece of the quilt. There are not always reports, but there is always praise, and we celebrate as if we received the answer we are still waiting for, believing every prayer will be answered. The quilt-in-progress always looks amazing because there are all different colors, and the beautiful red stands out as answered prayers. It is a perfect design and a perfect quilt because we serve and pray to a perfect God.[4] This is a one-of-a-kind quilt for a one-of-a-kind God who knows what we need and when we need it. We are prayer warriors together with Jesus who have the awesome task and honor of doing ministry with the[5] Holy Spirit in the beauty and sweetness of everlasting hope. We gather[6] in unity. We are one in giving and one in receiving, but we are individually used by the will of God in different ways, in answers, in[7] directions, and in the path set before us.

Our eyes may never meet, or maybe they will, but our spirits and hearts are in coordination and cooperation in one unit of love, with undivided hearts; a oneness for the blessed and graced opportunity to come to the throne of grace for each other, for loved ones, and the needs of others throughout the world. In cooperation, we conquer with faith over fear and hope over despair. It is more than a once-unmet dream, but the vision of hope manifesting, blooming in the wondrous Glory of His blessings. The Lord moves mountains[8] and opens doors that are otherwise thought to be closed or inaccessible. When the Lord opens doors, they cannot be shut, unless by the One who has all power.

Praying

> Here is my servant, whom I have chosen, my beloved, with whom my soul is well pleased. Matthew 12:18

There[9] are a vast number of people who are unaware of their need for the results the power of prayer can produce. God[9] made no mistake in giving this awesome assignment to those of us who are devoted to praying for others and reaching the needs of those hurting, lost, and distraught. The Lord has chosen wisely with great love and power those who accept this mission for the kingdom of God. Those who are unaware of the power of prayer always need hope when things are not going great or even good. God always knows what their needs are, and so, we pray in season and out of season.[10] Prayers are for all the precious souls throughout the world who may not be known by name. Mothers who have children hungry and undernourished, those with mental anguish from abusive people in their lives, and those harassed and treated unjustly by racism and victimization for being human.

When we say, "Let the elders plant the trees in which they will never sit in its shade," we are planting prayers in hope[11] for generations to come. The hope of prayer lies in our hearts and minds for the present age and many years to come. Our prayers are actionable measures for a better today and a hopeful tomorrow. They are for[12] courage and strength, as the elders pray for the young. It is for the older generation to embrace a new day, and the challenges faced today in every aspect of life, from jobs to housing, from diversity and inclusion to fairness and equity for all. God knows how to send prayer warriors to fight on the battlefield with praise and prayer.

The Perfect Quilt
As We Pray Together as One

Lord, where You are, we pray. Meet us, precious savior, while we quilt together. And as you do the weaving, Lord God, pour your spirit into this quilt of prayer intercessors. We submit to your call to pray. We gather Lord, to bring wondrous glory to your precious and holy name. To you, we bring honor and reverence for who you are, the highest esteemed greatness, for your loving kindness beyond measure, and your unconditional forgiveness for the sins of this world. You love us because you made us in your image.

Some of us are close friends, and some of us only know each other because you brought us together at this time of prayer. We once saw one another for the first time, but now we are one in you as we seek you in this place and sew our threads into beautiful cloth.

The quilting begins to form in the call to you, Lord, we gather in all shapes and of many needs, hopes, and struggles, the not-so-strong holding the not strong at all, the stronger holding the strong, and the strongest holding the weakest. In you, the power is released, full of your awesome grace, mercy, and love. Thank you, Lord, we love you. Amen.

1. Romans 15:13, 5:4, 12:12 (NRSVUE)
2. I Corinthians 12:4; Acts 4:24
3. Genesis 37:3
4. Psalms 139:14
5. Galatians 3:5; Jude 1:20
6. Acts 4:24
7. Proverbs 2:9
8. Mark 11:24; Matthew 17:20
9. Matthew 9:36
10. II Timothy 4:2
11. Acts 14:23
12. Joshua 1:9; Deuteronomy 31:6

A Mother and wife, Rev. Ellen Carter-Haygood is a passionate and dedicated supporter in ministry. Her journey focuses on her practical walk of faith in everyday life that carries into any ministry work she encounters. Her belief in loving God's children and sharing Jesus is intentional, radical, and consistent. The light she carries to many along the way helps others see the path of hope by showing the way in this journey of life with joy, conviction, purpose, and hope is beyond the obstacles that only attempt to block the flow of love and hope for a brighter tomorrow, with gratitude for every day. Her prayer is in Col 3:12 and Ps. 107:21 to stay humble, strong, loving, and grateful to the Lord for love and so many blessings.

Behind the Fog – the Word of God

Ruby Warthen

Looking out of my window, I could see nothing but fog.

It was thick and heavily hung in the atmosphere.

Once the sun came shining through, the fog lifted.

In my spirit, I heard the Lord say, "There will be times in life when your faith will be tested." James 1:3 says, "Knowing this, that the trying of your faith worketh patience." Keep the faith! There will be times in life when you will lack direction. In times like these, read Proverbs 3:5-6:

> Trust in the Lord with all thine heart and lean not unto thine own understanding. In all thy ways acknowledge Him, and He shall direct thy paths.

Trust Him!

There will be times in life when the fog of tribulation, the fog of sickness and disease, persecution, poverty, and even death will be present in our lives. Know that Jesus is on the other side, behind the fog. He will ensure your victory! He will work everything out for your good. Hallelujah!

Read Romans 8:28:

> And we know that all things work together for good to them that love God, to them who are called according to His purpose.

> *Father, in Jesus' name, we thank You for always being with us through every circumstance of life. We thank You for Your word that we can depend on for guidance and victory in the end. Thank You that You will be on the other side, just behind the fog!*

Scripture References: James 1:3, Proverbs 3:5-6, Romans 8:28

The Book

I want to share with you today about *The Book*.

This book is the world's number one bestseller. This book is filled with everything that involves mankind from Genesis to Revelation. It tells us of a plan that a loving Father has for His creation.

In fact, we see evidence of this in John 3:16:

> For God so loved the world that He gave His only begotten Son, that whosoever believeth in Him should not perish but have everlasting life.

Everything that we will ever need has already been provided for us through Jesus Christ, God's Son. This was accomplished through Christ's death, burial, and resurrection! Hallelujah! The Book, or the Bible, is God's Manufacturer's Manual. It will navigate or guide you all the way from earth to heaven. Now that's good news!

If this book were ever taken out of the world, darkness would prevail, because the light would be gone.

> Thy word is a lamp unto my feet and a light unto my path. Psalm 119:105

How many of us have taken the time to hide the Word in our hearts? When we put the words of This Book into our hearts, they will be there forever! Why not start today? Read, study, meditate on, and obey it—the Bible, God's word to you!

> For the word of God is quick and powerful, and sharper than any two-edged sword, piercing even to the dividing asunder of soul and spirit, and of the joints and marrow, and is a discerner of the thoughts and intents of the heart. Hebrews 4:12

Father, we thank You for Your book, the Bible. May it always be the first and final authority in our lives. Thank You, Lord, that Your word gives us direction for each day. It is a lamp unto our feet and a light unto our path.

In Jesus' name, Amen!

Ruby Warthen was called of God to teach the Word of God as a teenager. God has mandated her to minister His Word to bruised, broken, and hurting women. She studied theology at Manhattan Bible Institute in NYC. She co-pastored with her now-deceased husband, Wade, for six years in Oklahoma. She is currently facilitating two intercessory prayer lines: Widows Among Us and Keep Hope Alive.

Our Code Foundation

Dr. Elsie L. Scott

> That is why we never give up. Though our bodies are dying, our spirits are being renewed every day. For our present troubles are small and won't last very long. Yet they produce for us a glory that vastly outweighs them and will last forever! So, we don't look at the troubles we can see now; rather, we fix our gaze on things that cannot be seen. For the things we see now will soon be gone, but the things we cannot see will last forever. 2 Corinthians 16-18

When I started preparing this meditation, I was working on a totally different theme, but I was driven to write something that could be inspirational to people who are going through hard times, especially those who are concerned about the divisions they see in this country. I was led to go back to the period when the country became so split that a civil war was declared. On April 12, 1861, the Civil War started after the Confederate states seceded from the Union and fired on Fort Sumter.

Confederate soldiers signed up to defend their way of life, which included the enslavement of people who were stolen from Africa, and the enslavement of their descendants.

What do ministers preach when both sides feel that God is on their side, and they are doing the right thing?

Biblical historians have drawn conclusions by reading sermons preached and prayers prayed during the Civil War. Some preachers tried to take a safe route by merely praying for the President of the United States. But they found themselves being blasted by members of their congregation who supported the Confederacy. Others drew from biblical passages related to support for political leaders and country.

One minister in Albany, NY, preached a sermon entitled, "The Duty of the Citizen During These Times," on April 20, 1861. He stressed the Christian duty of loyalty to country.

Another minister who refused to pray for the US president found himself without a church after the Union army took the church building and converted it into a hospital.

Other ministers tried to avoid showing any favoritism in their sermons by trying to ignore what was happening around them.

Still others used the Bible to justify slavery and portrayed slave owners as protecting African people who they saw as less than human.

We find no difference today when many religious leaders are not supportive of helping the less fortunate in society. Many are ignoring the poor in order to garner favors from political leaders.

They should read a popular prayer that has been passed down from the Civil War era. No one knows the name of this Confederate soldier. But the prayer is often cited:

> *I asked God for strength, that I might achieve; I was made weak, that I might learn humbly to obey. I asked for health, that I might do greater things; I was given infirmity, that I might do better things. I asked for riches, that I might be happy; I was given poverty, that I might be wise. I asked for power, that I might have the praise of men; I was given weakness, that I might feel the need of God. I asked for all things, that I might enjoy life; I was given life that I might enjoy all things. I got nothing that I asked for, but everything I hoped for. Almost despite myself, my unspoken prayers were answered. I am among all men most richly blessed. Author unknown*

The Civil War presented many ethical dilemmas for the white people who lived during that era. Today, one of the ethical dilemmas being faced by political and business leaders is support for D.E.I. (Diversity, Equity, and Inclusion). DEI programs and initiatives are being interpreted as evil rather than as principles that could improve society.

As a society, we are facing decisions regarding what is right and what is wrong.

I remember teaching ethical dilemmas to a class of police cadets.

Teaching that class made me realize that things are no longer good, bad, right, or wrong. These young people had grown up in an era of middle grounds when the decision of right and wrong often involved the statement, 'It depends on the circumstances."

I could understand that sometimes there is a middle ground, but these young people struggled over circumstances where, based on my upbringing and religious training, there was a definite right or wrong answer. I worried that they would get killed while they struggled to figure out what was right and wrong.

I tried to stress to them the importance of having a personal moral code that governs your life. This code would dictate the appropriate action, and the individual would not have to try to remember what they were taught in Sunday School or the academy, or what the criminal code says.

Those of us who are Christians have the foundation for our code. That is the Bible.

If we were confronted by John Quiñones from the television show, we would not be embarrassed because we would not have to struggle to figure out "What We Would Do."

O Lord, give me strength to resist the temptations that are presented to me.

Give me discernment to know the difference between good and evil.

Help me to have faith, wisdom, and courage to make right decisions.

Give me the ability to overcome, to rise above my troubles.

Help me to fix my gaze on things that cannot be seen. For the things we see now will soon be gone, but the things we cannot see will last forever.

We pray in Jesus' name.

Amen.

Dr. Elsie L. Scott, a Stewart Emeritus at Metropolitan African Methodist Episcopal Church, Washington, DC

Leslie K. Powell Pitchford

St. John 11:35 displays our LORD and Savior JESUS, showing emotions and grief regarding a situation he knew would take place and would be rectified at the appointed time. Lives would be changed, grieving would cease, and another accomplishment would be completed within his ministry, letting us know all things are possible for those who believe, even in tests and trials. Remember, they don't last always, just for a season.

"Get up out of that GRAVE!" Lazarus heard his name. That is powerful because this was personal; he was called by his name and knew JESUS' VOICE! I believe there was more than one Lazarus buried, but the Lazarus Jesus called heard His voice and came forth. If Jesus were to call your name, would you be able to hear? Or would you be occupied with your favorite nouns - people, places, and things? Are you grieving over something GOD himself removed out of your life so you can come forth in your due season? If so, why are you allowing that to hold you down?

Listen, I have found myself in many ditches and buried situations because I put myself there by not consulting GOD. Instead, I listened to individuals give their opinion on things GOD never had envisioned for me, about a plan or a relationship, traveling, or moving to different places without referring to Proverbs 3:5,6. You get it. Trust GOD first with all you have or desire. Sometimes, family and friends may mean well, but we can't let them influence us over what GOD told us or showed us in a dream, vision, or prophecy regarding our lives. You may be waiting for a financial answer from the Lord, and it seems like it will never be answered, but have faith and wait on your season to receive that overflow of blessing and answers because it will surely come to pass.

At this point in the scripture, even Jesus had someone try to speak doubt into his ear. Martha, Lazarus's sister, captured his heart because she was grieving for her brother. She stated in St. John 11:39 her doubting bullet points. 1. He stinketh. 2. It's been four days. Be aware of who is speaking in your ear during testing times or when you are believing GOD for something in your life. JESUS said in St. John 10:10, "The thief comes only to steal, kill, and destroy." Remember also, timing can bring challenging moments when we are believing GOD for something. I always refer to my favorite scripture among many, John 14:1, "Let not your heart be troubled: ye believe in GOD, believe also in me." Get the substance of Faith working during your fight and rise with the power of the word of GOD!

Ecclesiastes 3, "To everything there is a season." Know your time! Jesus knew the timing was coming when Lazarus would be called forth. God knew you before you were in your mother's womb. Believe me, He has your season planned for you as well. Something great and special will happen if you have confidence and faith; everything you ask according to His will, be it unto you. He will order your steps if you let Him, don't go ahead of yourself into a strange land that wasn't scripted for you! Rejoice that you know his voice; your faith and trust in GOD will get you out of every hindrance the enemy tries to bring!

> *Father GOD, in the name of JESUS, it is my will to surrender to you everything that I am and everything that I'm striving to be. I open the deepest recesses of my heart and invite your Holy Spirit to dwell inside of me. I offer you my life, heart, mind, body, soul, spirit, all my hopes, plans, and dreams. I surrender to you my past, present, and future problems, habits, character defects, attitudes, livelihood, resources, finances, medical coverage, occupation, and all my relationships.*

A woman of unwavering faith, Mrs. Leslie Pitchford dedicates her life as a servant and prophetess of God, a path she embraced wholeheartedly on September 28, 1986, when she accepted Jesus Christ into her life. Beyond her spiritual calling, Leslie is a loving wife and the proud mother of two beautiful daughters. Her testimony of healing is truly miraculous, having overcome two forms of Stage 4 and 5 cancers. Professionally, Leslie contributes her expertise within the finance sector.

The Fullness of God

Earnestine Porter

> [that you] ...may be able to comprehend with all saints what is the breadth, and length, and depth, and height; and to know the love of Christ, which passeth knowledge, that ye might be filled with all the fullness of God. Hebrews 4:12

I am fascinated by this passage of Scripture because, as a child, I hungered to live a life pleasing to God, in spite of the fact that I had no knowledge of the Person of Jesus Christ. I knew that there was something in knowing Him that was far beyond what my childlike mind could ever visualize.

This hunger persisted throughout my teen years into adulthood. During this process, I sensed that if I desire to live for God, I must first build a relationship with Jesus Christ. So here comes Ephesians 3 and in particular verses 18-19. The floodgates of making Jesus all I desire as a child have been laid bare for me, that little girl with "The Hunger for God."

Ephesians 3:18-19 is an essential part of a larger prayer by Apostle Paul for the Ephesians' church, in which he prays that they may be strengthened in their inner being by the Spirit of God and that Christ may dwell in their hearts through faith. Paul also prayed that the Ephesians, along with all believers, may come to a deep understanding of the love of Christ, which surpasses human knowledge. This knowledge extends to all people regardless of their background, and also for them to be filled with the "fullness of God." The fullness of God can be understood as the presence of God's Spirit, who empowers and strengthens all believers in their faith.

To conclude, Ephesians 3:18-19 is a powerful prayer that gives believers a deep understanding of the immeasurable love of Christ and allows them to be filled with the fullness of God. Apostle Paul uses this prayer as a reminder to all believers to seek a deep and intimate relationship with their Creator and to experience the "fullness of His love" in their lives.

> *Prayer to Know the Fullness of God*
>
> *Ephesians 3:14-21*
>
> *For this reason I bow my knees to the Father [f]of our Lord Jesus Christ, from whom the whole family in heaven and earth is named, that He would grant you, according to the riches of His glory, to be strengthened with might through His Spirit in the inner man, that Christ may dwell in your hearts through faith; that you, being rooted and grounded in love, may be able to comprehend with all the saints what is the width and length and depth and height—to know the love of Christ which passes knowledge; that you may be filled with all the fullness of God. Now to Him who is able to do exceedingly abundantly above all that we ask or think, according to the power that works in us, to Him be glory in the church by Christ Jesus to all generations, forever and ever. Amen.*

Earnestine Porter, aka Elder Tina, is a resident of South Carolina. She was educated in Berkeley County Public Schools, where she received her training in cosmetology.

Upon relocating north, she attended Brown Business School in Jamaica, New York, Evangelical Bible Institute, and Good News Bible School in New Jersey.

Over the years, God called her to serve in many ministries as a prayer intercessor, an Elder, a Missionary, a substitute Sunday school teacher, and in many more capacities. Email: agappe1@aol.com

Renewed Like an Eagle

Evangelist Ida Flowers

The Lord satisfies your mouth with good things so that your youth is renewed like an eagle's. (Psalm 103:5) He desires to renew us, body, soul, and spirit. As we align our lives with His divine principles, we find ourselves strengthened and transformed in every area.

Let us explore how to offer our bodies to God in service, steward our health wisely, and embrace the abundance He has for us.

We are called to present our bodies as a living sacrifice, holy and acceptable to God. Our bodies are the temple of the Holy Spirit, and caring for them is an act of worship. This means not only offering our physical strength for God's service but also treating our bodies with reverence. When we surrender our physical well-being to God, it opens the door for Him to work through us unhindered by poor health or lack of vitality.

Third John 1 and 2 remind us that God's desire is for us to prosper and be in health, just as our souls prosper. Physical health and spiritual health go hand in hand. As we draw closer to the Lord, we should also strive to bring our physical lives in alignment with His will, cultivating healthy eating habits, practicing self-care, and acknowledging that our well-being reflects His glory. Prosperity in every area of life is God's promise, and that includes the health of our bodies.

God created the earth and filled it with nourishment for our bodies. In the book of Genesis (1:29), it states that God gave us herbs for the service of man, also, plants and fruit for food, each containing the nutrients needed for a healthy life. Instead of turning to processed, unhealthy options that drain our energy and harm our bodies, we should eat the foods God created for our youthful vitality. Let God's food be the medicine that sustains us, fueling our bodies with life-giving energy, so that we can thrive in the work He has called us to.

Being intercessors, we must be strong. Since we take on the responsibility of intercession - lifting others up in prayer – it is vital that we remain physically healthy.

Spiritual warfare demands energy and endurance, and when we are fatigued or unwell, it can limit our ability to engage in the fight to pull down strongholds. A strong and healthy intercessor can stand in the gap with vigor, alert to the needs of others, and be responsive to the Spirit's promptings.

Living in alignment with God's will – spiritually, mentally, and physically – not only adds years to our lives, but life to our years. Quality of life matters to God. A life well-lived for His glory is vibrant, purposeful, and enduring. As we care for our bodies, we are better equipped to fulfill our divine callings, serve others effectively, and have a lasting impact on the world. By honoring the Lord with our health, we extend our capacity to enjoy the fullness of His blessings.

As we reflect on Psalm 103:5 – Who satisfies our mouth with good things so that our youth is renewed like an eagle's – let us thank God for the way He sustains us and renews our strength. Commit today to offer your body as a living sacrifice, to steward your health, and enjoy the blessing of vitality that God has for you.

Say this prayer aloud:

> *Father, I offer my body to You as a living sacrifice. I acknowledge that it is Your temple, and I ask for Your grace to honor You with my health, my actions, and my service. Use me for Your purposes and renew my strength (youth) as I serve You. I lay down every weakness, weariness, and limitation before You. Renew me physically, emotionally, and spiritually so that I may be used fully for Your glory. In the mighty name of Jesus. Amen!*

Psalm 103:5, Psalm 104:14, Gen 1:29, I Cor 6:19, 3 John 1:2, Ezekiel 22:30

Evangelist Ida Flowers is an intercessor, prayer warrior, and aspiring health coach. She formerly co-pastored Revival Fellowship Church in Plainfield, New Jersey, with her late husband, Bishop Kenneth Flowers, Sr., for 15 years. Evangelist Flowers lives a life of faith. She can be contacted at chooselife32@gmail.com.

Making a Transition from Belief to Faith: Strategies of Heaven

Sermon Excerpt of Paster Kenneth A. Flowers, Jr. lovingly shared by his wife, Min. Renee S. Flowers

> And He spake a parable unto them to this end, that men ought always to pray, and not to faint.
> Luke 18:1-8

Shall not God Avenge His Elect?

Pastor Kenny pointed out that we are "the elect of GOD, who cry day and night to HIM." Then he posed a question: "Are you a day and night crier? Are you constantly before HIS face?"

Jesus gave this parable: The unjust judge thought, "If I don't do something about this woman's issue, she is going to keep coming." Her faith was evident because she was determined—even if she had to come every day—to put everything else aside to receive the results she sought. The judge recognized this persistence.

The Bible says that the people of GOD should set their faces like flint—focused, unwavering, and steadfast in their faith. Just like the widow in the parable who continually sought justice, we must persist in prayer, believing that GOD will answer. Jesus concluded, "I tell you; He will avenge them speedily. Nevertheless, when the Son of Man comes again, shall He find faith on the earth?"

Belief vs. Faith: Understanding the Difference

Many people assume that belief and faith are the same, but while they are related, they are not identical. What is belief? People often say, "I believe GOD can heal. I believe GOD will save my loved ones. I believe GOD will help me out of my situation." But they stop there. Belief acknowledges what GOD can do, but faith takes action.

Faith Is Acting on What You Believe

Say it with me: "Faith is moving or acting on what I believe." When you first made your confession to receive JESUS as Lord and Savior, you prayed the Sinner's Prayer. The Bible says, "If you confess with your mouth the Lord Jesus and believe in your heart, you shall be saved." It starts with belief. But after salvation, you must walk out what you believe—you must grow.

Many people remain in belief mode without transitioning into faith. You can tell by what they say and what they fail to do. Faith is demonstrated through action. For example, you may believe that GOD can save the world, your community, and your family, but if you never act—if you never step out to share the love of Christ—then you are still in belief and have not transferred to faith.

Faith in Action: The Woman with the Issue of Blood

When people touched Jesus, He didn't say, "My faith has healed you." Instead, He said, "Woman, your faith has made you whole."

She was willing to stop standing in belief and take action, even though it was uncomfortable. She pushed through the crowd because she knew Jesus had the answer.

I can imagine the pain she endured—her body frail from years of suffering. But when she reached Him, she declared, "If I could just touch the hem of His garment, I KNOW I will be healed." She acted on what she believed, and she was healed.

Jesus, feeling the power leave Him, asked, "Who touched me?" The disciples, confused, replied, "Master, many are touching you." But Jesus knew that someone had drawn power from Him through faith.

Moving from Belief to Faith in Prayer

Belief is good, but you must not stay there. You must move into faith by acting on what you believe. When you pray, do so with faith—believing that GOD will answer. Faith means you pray with expectation, knowing that what you believe will come to pass for you and your loved ones. Does that make sense? Give the LORD a praise!

The Strategies of Heaven

Colossians 1:9-11 & 1 Samuel 30 tell us that GOD has a strategy for every situation. Heaven operates on divine strategies, and faith activates them.

We must understand:
- The knowledge of HIS will.
- The wisdom to act on that knowledge.
- The spiritual understanding of what we are facing.

GOD Has a Plan for You

GOD has assigned each of us a purpose. You were created to solve a problem. Jesus was sent to solve the problem of sin. And just as GOD had a strategy for Jesus, He has a strategy for you. Your life is not a mistake—GOD planned it before you were born. So, no matter what you're going through, remember: GOD is not surprised. He has already designed a strategy for your breakthrough.

Operating by Faith, Not Just Belief

When the blind man was healed, the disciples asked, "Who sinned, this man or his parents?" Jesus responded, "Neither. This happened so that the glory of GOD could be revealed." The same applies to you. Your situation is not meant to destroy you—it is an opportunity for GOD's glory to be seen in your life.

So, we must move beyond belief and operate by faith.

Final Encouragement: Faith Requires Action

The Bible says, "Occupy until I come." This does not mean simply taking up space but standing firm in faith and doing what GOD has called you to do—even if you don't see the results immediately. Faith requires patience, endurance, and joy. Remember, GOD is strategic. He has already planned your victory. Say it with me: "I will move from belief to faith. I will pray with faith, act on what I believe, and trust in GOD's strategy for my life."

Hallelujah! Give the LORD a praise!

Pastor Kenneth A. Flowers Jr., born March 20, 1970, in East Orange, NJ, faithfully served in ministry for over three decades. He accepted Jesus Christ as his Savior at the age of 16, and he received the gift of the Holy Ghost shortly after, igniting a lifelong passion for intercession, worship, and the demonstration of God's power.

He was ordained in the early 1990s by his father, the late Apostle Kenneth A. Flowers Sr., and later served as Youth Pastor and Associate Pastor at Living Waters Worship Center in Plainfield, NJ, under Pastors James and Emma Spann. In 2009, Pastor Kenneth founded **All Heart Ministries** *alongside his wife, Co-Pastor Renée Flowers, with a vision to minister life, hope, and strength to the total man. His commitment to revival, community outreach, and youth development was evident through his leadership, mentorship, and creative approach to ministry.*

A worshiper at heart, Pastor Kenneth was also a published children's book author and passionate advocate for the arts and youth empowerment. He partnered with various faith-based and civic organizations to uplift the city of Plainfield and beyond.

Pastor Kenneth was a devoted husband to Renée and a proud father to their daughter, Ketzia Renée Simone Flowers, who was the joy of his life.

A Prayer for Salvation

Heavenly Father, according to Ephesians 1:7, in You we have redemption through Jesus' blood, the forgiveness of sins, according to the riches of Your grace. Therefore, I come to You in the Name of Jesus, asking You for forgiveness of my sins and receiving Your forgiveness. Your Word says, "Whosoever shall call on the name of the Lord shall be saved" Acts 2:21. I am calling on You. I pray and ask Jesus to come into my heart and be Lord over my life according to Romans 10:9-10, "If thou shalt confess with thy mouth the Lord Jesus, and shalt believe in thine heart that God hath raised him from the dead, thou shalt be saved." I do that now. I confess that Jesus is Lord, and I believe in my heart that God raised Him from the dead.

If you have prayed this prayer, welcome to the family of God.

Congratulations on making the most important decision of your life—accepting Jesus Christ as your Lord and Savior! This is just the beginning of a beautiful journey of faith, growth, and purpose.

One of the next important steps is to find and join a local, Bible-believing church. A church family will help nurture your faith, support you through prayer and fellowship, and guide you as you grow in your relationship with God. In community, you'll discover what it means to walk with Christ daily, be encouraged by other believers, and find your place in God's purpose for your life.

Don't walk this journey alone—connect with a local congregation where you can be loved, taught, and empowered. God designed us to grow together. Welcome to the family of faith!

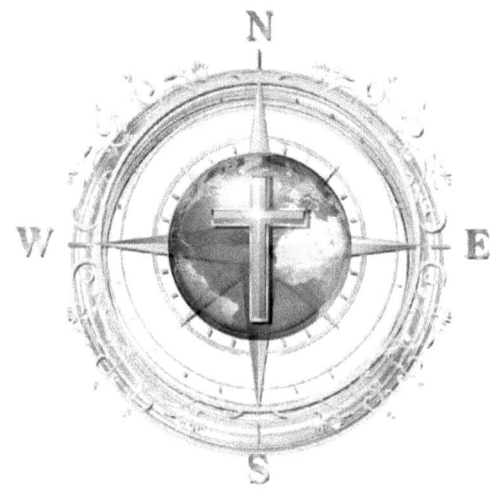

Global Compass
Prayer Ministries Inc.

www.ingramcontent.com/pod-product-compliance
Lightning Source LLC
Chambersburg PA
CBHW050519100526
44581CB00001B/39